CAROLINE NORTON'S DEFENSE

CAROLINE NORTON'S DEFENSE

English Laws for Women in the
Nineteenth Century

by

Caroline Norton

Introduction by
Joan Huddleston

Academy
Chicago

Academy Chicago
425 N. Michigan Ave.
Chicago, IL 60611
All rights reserved
Printed and bound in the USA

Library of Congress Cataloging in Publication Data

Norton, Caroline Sheridan, 1808-1877.
    Caroline Norton's defense.

    Reprint. Originally published: English laws for women
in the nineteenth century. London, 1854.
    1. Women—Legal status, laws, etc.—Great Britain.
2. Husband and wife—Great Britain. I. Title.
KD734.N67 1982   346.4201'34   82-1823
ISBN 0-915864-87-8   344.206134   AACR2
ISBN 0-915864-88-6 (pbk.)

INTRODUCTION

> From time immemorial, changes in the laws of nations have been brought about by individual examples of oppression. Such examples *cannot* be unimportant, for they are, and ever will be, the little hinges on which the great doors of justice are made to turn.
>
> [Caroline Norton, *Letter to the Queen*]

The cause of women's liberation was no exception to this rule, particularly in the early 19th century before women organized themselves into activist groups. And Caroline Norton's own example is a case in point. Her personal sorrows and the difficulties of her marital situation were the spur to her active campaigning for the improvement of the common lot of married women at that time. She sought initially to improve her own life through changes in the laws that restricted her but the results were to alleviate the problems of many others in similar situations, and the legal reforms she supported and helped to bring about were the beginnings of the massive changes in the legal position of women which snowballed through the later years of the century. However, she did not believe in the principal advocacy of equality, or even in the banding together of women in revolutionary groups. She did not believe in the equality of men and women at all:

> The natural position of woman is inferiority to man. Amen! That is a thing of God's appointing, not of man's devising. I believe it sincerely, as part of my religion. I never pretended to the wild and ridiculous doctrine of equality.
>
> [*Letter to the Queen*]

I

She sought only to improve the methods by which men could protect women, and to establish legal remedies if this protection should fail. She fought not a generalized rebellion against men (indeed she sought assistance from her male relatives and friends in all her troubles), but she fought the inconsistencies, meannesses and, on occasion, brutalities of her husband, using as her most powerful weapon her literary talents. And so she helped the woman's cause, a feminist *malgré lui.* She played a large part in bringing about the Infant Custody Bill, caused certain reforms to be added to the Matrimonial Causes Act, and created the climate in which discussions could begin towards the Married Women's Property Acts; all major improvements to the deplorable conditions under which women were non-persons with no legal rights, no legal status, and were classed with slaves and idiots as outside the law and able to take no advantage of it.

Although she was born in 1808, Caroline Sheridan's background, and to an extent her personality, belonged to the 18th century. She inherited from her playwright grandfather, Richard Brinsley Sheridan, her wit and charm, and was always a striking figure. Her rash and impulsive actions brought her a reputation for notoriety that clung even when her marital wrongs should have brought her sympathy. She would have attracted a good deal more sympathy if she had submissively accepted her sad fortune or allowed her male relatives to seek on her behalf to rectify the situation, whether it was a matter of gaining access to her children or winning financial support from her estranged husband. Instead she chose to enter the public arena herself.

Her father was Thomas Sheridan, only son of the playwright and his first wife Elizabeth Lynley. Born into the exciting period of his father's social and artistic success, he grew up educated to no career, with no financial independence. He eloped with Henrietta Callander against the wishes of her well-born Scottish family who disapproved of his charm, his lack of money, his connection with the theatre and his father's links with the Prince Regent and the fast-living Whig set which gathered at Holland House. But theirs was a happy marriage and they became a close and united family in

II

spite of the slow decline of the family fortunes. The three daughters Helen, Caroline and Georgiana, in particular remained mutually devoted friends throughout their lives. Thomas Sheridan's early death in 1816, of consumption, inherited from his mother's family, left his widow with seven small children to maintain. But strangely enough his death brought them greater comfort and security: his father's artistic fame persuaded his political patrons to find the widow and her large family a free 'grace and favour' apartment at Hampton Court where they settled in reasonable peace and contentment.

All but Caroline, that is, whose literary bent and tempestuous character marked her out from the others: it was decided she needed the discipline of boarding school. It was here, in Surrey, that she met her future husband, George Norton.

He was the younger brother and heir of Lord Grantley of Wonersh, a landowner of some means, though George himself had little money of his own, and few talents. He was wildly attracted to young Caroline and declared that he wished to marry her. She was removed from his society because of her youth and brought back to London.

At 17 she was launched into her first season, the marriage market of London society. But although she was recognised as a noted beauty, she received no offers of marriage that year. Her good looks could not compensate for a lack of dowry, and for the taint of theatricality associated with her family. There was no other possibility for a girl than marriage and motherhood. There were honourable exceptions, of course, like Harriet Martineau; but Caroline never saw herself as remaining single and independent, nor thought that she might support herself as a writer. Her elder sister Helen married without love but was happy in the married state.

Thus, when George Norton renewed his proposal, she had little alternative but to accept. She did not love him—indeed she scarcely knew him—but he was presentable. Apart from anything else, she knew she must cease to be a financial burden on the family before her sister Georgiana was launched into her first season the following year.

So in July, 1826, they married, when Caroline was 19 and

III

George 26. Caroline could enter fully into social life, acquire a circle of friends and visitors, and even indulge in discreet friendships with the opposite sex. Unfortunately the temperamental differences between her and her husband were to deny her much of the comfort and pleasure this prospect afforded. Their political differences too were to cause dissension, particularly as London debated the broadening of the franchise that was to culminate in the Great Reform Bill of 1832. The debate split families and friends, dividing society into violently opposed camps. Caroline's Whiggish support for the Bill and George's Tory opposition to it added much bitterness to their already divided household. But the more basic problems were personal. George always remained physically attracted to her, and she always wanted to love and respect him as the father of her children, but her fiery temper and his stolid sullenness, her verbal defiance and his physical violence made their life together almost unbearable.

Caroline cannot be regarded as blameless; she found it difficult to accept any discipline, let alone the conventions which gave George unlimited powers over her while allowing nothing for her strength of spirit and superior abilities. Things were made worse by the support George received from his relatives, in particular Lord Grantley, and a Miss Vaughan from whom George hoped to inherit. They encouraged him in his petty cruelties. Caroline's family, too, rushed into the fray. It was probably inevitable that the witty and engaging Sheridans would join in despising the dull conservatism of the Nortons, but it did nothing to help the couple sort out their life together.

It is by no means clear, however, whether anything at all could have helped to improve the situation. Even if George had had an occupation appropriate to his interests, if he had retained his seat in Parliament or inherited his brother's estate, instead of having to depend on a political job secured for him by Caroline; even if their money situation had been significantly better than it was, there were still factors which would have divided them. Her lack of a dowry would always be a sore spot in their relationship; as were the higher social standing of the Sheridan ladies. With Georgiana marrying

IV

Lord Seymour, the heir to the Duke of Somerset, and with their friendship with Court ladies (Caroline dedicated her *The Undying One* in 1830 to the Duchess of Clarence who became Queen Adelaide that same year) George was made to feel that he was lower in rank and social respect than his wife.

At all events, by 1835 the Nortons with their three sons were a very unhappy family, short of affection for each other, short of money but with an excess of outside interference and even manipulation. George had been elected to Parliament in 1826 and might legitimately have expected his wife to use her social skills on behalf of his Tory party, but, on the contrary, she openly defied her husband by actively working for the Whigs in support of the Reform Bill.

In 1830 Parliament was dissolved on the death of George IV and in the ensuing election George lost his seat and his income. Caroline's literary career brought in a steady income but not enough to cover all the expenses of a growing family and a hectic round of social engagements. She rallied to George's support and contacted her political friends to try to persuade them to find employment for him. Among those who responded to her appeals was Lord Melbourne.

William Lamb, Lord Melbourne, as Home Secretary, had control over a great deal of political patronage and found a position for George as magistrate in one of the police courts. One result of this appointment was a closer friendship between Caroline and Melbourne, which was later to prove harmful to them both, but in particular to her. Melbourne became a frequent visitor at Caroline's home in Storey's Gate, just across St. James's Park from his office in Downing Street, and from Buckingham Palace. His wife, Lady Caroline Lamb, had soon after their marriage devoted herself ostentatiously to Lord Byron, and she became notorious for her escapades. Her husband received society's sympathy and remained touchingly loyal to her, forgiving her eccentric behaviour on many occasions, and when her personality became more and more erratic, received her back into his home and supported her till her death in 1828. In the same year he became Lord Melbourne on the death of his father. He had entered politics only in 1827 and was soon a popular

V

and accepted leader of political society, even surviving an accusation of adultery over his affair with Lady Brandon. Indeed it was well known that other ladies had received his attentions, though in many cases this amounted to no more than a desire for their sympathetic company.

When Caroline Norton joined his circle of women friends she was joining a group that was, seven years later, to include the young Queen Victoria herself. With the seventeen-year-old Queen, Melbourne began the most delicate and enduring of friendships which lasted till his death in 1848. There was nothing scandalous about that relationship, which clearly resembled that of uncle and niece, and there may have been nothing scandalous about his friendship with Caroline; but her impulsive nature, George's dangerous and ill-conditioned character, and the difficulties of the Nortons' marital situation should have led Melbourne to be more careful about involving her and himself in a social situation of a potentially explosive nature. But they did get involved with each other. He found her a warm-hearted and engaging companion, and she found him a wonderful antidote to George. She could respect and admire him, they were temperamentally suited, and she accepted him as a guide and counsellor as Queen Victoria was to do later.

George Norton seems to have accepted this friendship readily enough, possibly even encouraged it at first. As he owed the major part of his income to Melbourne he was not really in a position to do otherwise. But he was influenced by his relatives and their political allies to see it as a serious threat to his marital status. In March 1836, the Nortons had a quarrel about the children's visit to their uncle Brinsley. George had not been invited because the Sheridans could not forgive his brutal behaviour. Urged on by Miss Vaughan, George denied the boys their visit. Early next morning Caroline visited her sister to seek advice. While she was out of the house George bundled the children off to an unnamed destination. Caroline had them traced to Miss Vaughan's house where she herself went to seek them. She was denied access to them and received instead a barrage of abuse which was probably the accumulation of years of ill-feeling. She determined never to

VI

return to her husband's house and this time she did not retract her decision.

George responded first by declaring in the public press that he would no longer be liable for her debts—a most unnecessary and meaningless insult—and secondly by initiating divorce proceedings. In those days this was done by instituting a civil case for damages against a wife's lover for alienating her affections. Such cases were popularly known as "crim. cons." since they sought to prove that a man had had criminal conversations with another's wife, i.e. had committed adultery with her. George stunned London by naming Melbourne, who was then Prime Minister, as the guilty party, and thus ensured maximum notoriety for the case, and the greatest political disturbance possible. If Melbourne were to be found guilty he could be forced to resign and in a period of political instability this could bring the government down, to the delight of George's Tory friends.

Though many efforts were made to prevent it, the trial began on 22nd June, 1836. Caroline herself was not present and indeed she was not legally entitled to take part in it; she could neither defend herself nor have counsel to defend her. After all the fuss and sordid publicity, the jury found Melbourne innocent, without even withdrawing to consider their verdict. It was generally felt that the whole shabby affair was a plot created by political animus rather than a genuine feeling of outraged morality on the part of George Norton.

Although Melbourne emerged unscathed from the debacle, Caroline Norton was to face both short term and long term consequences that affected her life almost to its end. The failure of George's case meant that he could not divorce her because of insufficient grounds. Caroline could not divorce him because her return to him late in 1835 after a short separation had seemed to condone his brutality and possibly his infidelities. As so often in her life, her generously forgiving nature was her downfall.

So with divorce impossible all they could do was separate, and for this they had to agree terms. There were serious difficulties before those terms coud be established. Firstly, they were always dependent on the goodwill and integrity of

VII

both parties, and George had already proved himself to be extremely wayward, unreliable, and mean. Caroline had left all her possessions—clothes, books, jewellery—at Storey's Gate. But no approaches by herself or her brother could persuade George to return any of them to her. Secondly, these terms were not legally binding inasmuch as no legal contract could be entered into by a wife with her husband. Thirdly, the power to dictate the terms was the husband's right, even where the wife was the wronged party. Fourthly, the ecclesiastical court, the only divorce granting body, disapproved such a settlement. Therefore, the existence of such a settlement precluded the possibility of any future divorce.

In the end Caroline got an allowance of £300 a year but was still refused access to the children. Her literary career at this time was in the doldrums. She no longer edited *La Belle Assemblée* and *The English Annual* though she did publish *A Voice from the Factories* in November, 1836 in an effort to make money. Had it not been for the support of her brother and uncle she would have suffered financially, As it was, there is no doubt that throughout the four years that followed the trial she did suffer emotionally, deprived of any sight or knowledge of her sons, with the eldest in delicate health and the youngest only three years old. It was their loss that led her to campaign to change the laws which could allow such a barbaric situation.

She began by writing a pamphlet on the Infant Custody situation, and when she could not get her usual publisher, John Murray, to accept it, she had it printed privately at her own expense. In *Separation of Mother and Child by the Law of Custody of Infants Considered* she emphasized the iniquities of the current situation by which children born to married women became the property of their fathers from the moment of birth. It seemed anomalous that the mothers of illegitimate children could not be forbidden access to them while even "respectable" deserted wives might be forced to give up their children to their husbands' mistresses and never see them again. Caroline did not produce a fiery personal document on this occasion but a rational discussion of the existing state of affairs and the distress it caused. She met

VIII

with family opposition when she told them what she planned; they felt she should stay out of the public eye till all gossip about the trial died away. But she was determined to go ahead, and even distributed the pamphlet herself, circularising her friends in both Houses of Parliament. She lobbied all her political acquaintances, and faced the reactionary opposition she received with a quiet discretion that was unusual in her.

Through her friends, she met Sergeant Talfourd MP who had been junior defense counsel in the Melbourne Trial. In April 1837 he introduced an Infant Custody Bill but it met with various delays and then in mid-session Talfourd announced that he was postponing the measure till the next session because of its delicacy and importance. Some critics felt that the postponement was due to a temporary lull in the wrangling between the Nortons during which Caroline thought she might get to see her sons on a regular basis and that it was at her urging that Talfourd halted the Bill. Caroline denied in print that this was true.

Through 1837 and early 1838 she continued to seek the support of those of her friends who had political influence: the Bill needed all the support it could get. The most extraordinary arguments were raised against it—that the wives likely to want to use the Bill's provisions, that is, wives in conflict with their husbands, were the unchaste ones, and should therefore be denied maternal rights; and that the Bill would encourage wives to become licentious if the sanctions of the present system were withdrawn: this would constitute a danger to the fabric of society. Some opponents of the Bill went so far as to couple Caroline's name with Talfourd's in an offensive way, and here again Caroline found that her legal non-status prevented her from suing for libel. Ironically, only George could legally have sued on her behalf. In spite of all these arguments, the Bill passed the Commons in 1838; but it was rejected in the House of Lords and this meant that the whole process had to be begun again.

Undaunted, Caroline continued the fight, this time writing a *Plain Letter to the Lord Chancellor* under the pseudonym Pearse Stevenson, in the hopes that the absence of her name would allow rational argument to proceed.

In the following summer, 1839, the Bill became law and gave married mothers limited rights to their infant children, i.e. children under 7 years of age. The mothers had to prove themselves of spotless character, and had to petition the Lord Chancellor for a hearing before a special court which could grant what access it chose. It was a significant improvement though by no means perfect, and it was owed in large part to Caroline's steady work on its behalf.

Once the Bill was passed she immediately set about trying to get access to her own children, and made it clear to George and his lawyers that she would not hesitate to use material damaging to him if necessary. In the face of this George allowed the case to be settled out of court and grudgingly allowed her to see her boys in what she called "the most formal and comfortless manner." In 1842 her youngest son died in a riding accident. This tragedy brought the parents closer than they had been for years and George agreed to let her have the two remaining boys for six months of each year, provided she supported them financially. So after six years of separation she was able to have her two boys under her own roof again.

Caroline was now 34 years old, and for a brief period she had a measure of calm. She was restored to social favor, had been received at court by Queen Victoria in 1840; she was publishing successfully, in particular A Child of the Islands (1845), and doing some editing. She kept up with political writing too, publishing her Letters to the Mob during the Chartist activity in 1848. She kept a literary salon, having returned to Lord Melbourne's friendship after he lost office in 1841, and even though there were several deaths in the Sheridan family and she had the perpetual worry of her eldest son's poor health, she recognised that it was on the whole a restful period in her life.

Peace ended however when in 1848 George sought to get her consent to allow him to raise money on her marriage settlement. Under English law as it then stood, all the property of a girl became her husband's on the day she married, unless her father created a settlement on her by which the

X

husband was excluded from the use or enjoyment of her property unless she signed it over to him before witnesses. By 1848 George was in debt and needed the money badly. He used his eldest son as pleader on his behalf. Caroline could not bear to think of her son being used in this way, so she agreed immediately to his demands. It was characteristically imprudent of her to trust George in money matters, but she agreed to a legal deed which gave him power to raise money on her settlement in return for an increase in the allowance he made her. She should have known that no deed between husband and wife was legally valid; she was in effect dependent upon George's sense of honor to ensure that he carried out his part of the bargain. The ensuing story of financial and emotional entanglements is best left to her own account in the *Defense* itself.

On 18 August 1853 as a test case she allowed one of her creditors to sue her husband for payment of her debts. What happened in that trial and after it she herself tells us. In this document she supplies us with a vivid and moving account of a personal drama which powerfully illuminates the legal and other difficulties with which women of her class and period had to contend. Certainly hers is an individual case caused at least partly by the temperamental clash of the Nortons, but it brought to public notice in detailed form the appalling injustices that wives might suffer. It marked the start of the discussions that were to result in the Married Women's Property Acts of 1870, 1882, and 1893. It gave inspiration to many women who began to form themselves into activist groups to work for legal reform. One such woman was Barbara Leigh-Smith, later Mme Bodichon, who published in 1854 "A Brief Summary in Plain Language of the most important laws of England concerning women" which had far reaching effects at a time when law reform was in the air.

The last of Caroline's major endeavours in the field of women's rights was in 1855 when she published *A Letter to the Queen on Lord Cranworth's Marriage and Divorce Bill*. The divorce laws came under legal scrutiny at this time and were the cause of a good deal of heated discussion. Caroline's pamphlet was an important element in that discussion; it is one of her most powerfully written pieces. When the Matrimonial Causes Act of 1857 was passed, several of its clauses seemed to be the result of Caroline's contribution. Women henceforth as separated wives were protected in the possession of their earnings; they received maintenance as directed by the Court and no longer at their husband's whim; they were allowed as wives whether separated or not to inherit and bequeath property like single women; and as separated wives they gained the power of contract and could sue or be sued like single women. Here too we are in Caroline Norton's debt.

The rest of her life may be briefly told. She continued to bicker with George over money matters; she had to work hard at her literary career to support her grown-up sons. In 1859 the eldest boy, Fletcher, died of consumption and the shock told heavily upon her. George died in 1875 and this too shocked and distressed her, but in 1877 she married an old friend, Sir William Stirling-Maxwell. She died three months later on 15 June 1877.

It seems wrong to end an account of Caroline Norton with her old age and death. A more appropriate ending is surely the one she herself wrote in her 1855 *Letter to the Queen*:

My husband has taught me, by subpœnaing my publishers to account for my earnings, that my gift of writing was not meant for the purposes to which I have hitherto applied it. It was not intended that I should 'strive for peace and ensue it' through a life of much occasional bitterness and many unjust trials, nor that I should prove my literary ability by publishing melodies and songs for young girls and women to sing in happier homes than mine, or poetry and prose for them to read in leisure hours, or even please myself by better and more serious attempts to advocate the rights of the people or the education and interests of the poor. He has made me dream that it was meant for a higher and stronger purpose, that gift which came not from man, but from God! It was meant to enable me to rouse the hearts of others to examine into all the gross injustice of these laws, to ask the nation of gallant gentlemen whose countrywoman I am, for once to hear a woman's pleading on the subject. Not because I deserve more at their hands than other women. Well I know, on the contrary, how many hundreds, infinitely better than I—more pious, more patient, and less rash under injury—have watered their bread with tears! My plea to attention is that in pleading for myself I am able to plead for all these others. Not that my sufferings for my deserts are greater than theirs, but that I combine, with the fact of having suffered wrong, the power to comment on and explain the cause of that wrong, which few women are able to do. For this I believe God gave me the power of writing. To this I devote that power. I abjure all other writing till I see these laws altered. I care not what ridicule or abuse may be the result of that declaration. They who cannot bear ridicule and abuse are unfit and unable to advance any cause; and once more I deny that this is my personal cause—it is the cause of all the women of England. If I could be justified and happy to-morrow, I would still strive and labour in it; and if I were to die to-morrow, it would still be a satisfaction to me that I had so striven. Meanwhile my husband has a legal lien on the copyright of my works. Let him claim the copyright of this!

Joan Huddleston
University of Queensland
Australia
May 1, 1982

XIII

The Writings of Caroline Norton

The Sorrows of Rosalie and Other Poems. London: John Ebers, 1829.

The Undying One and Other Poems. London: H. Colburn & R. Bentley, 1830.

Poems and Sketches in *The Court Magazine* and *The Belle Assemblée* for 1832-34.

Poems in the *English Annual* for 1834-35.

The Wife, and Woman's Reward. London: Saunders & Otley, 1835.

Poems in *The Keepsake* for 1836.

A Voice from the Factories. London: John Murray, 1836.

Separation of Mother and Child by the Law of Custody of Infants considered. Printed privately by J. Ridgway, 1837.

A Plain letter to the Lord Chancellor, by Pearce Stevenson. Printed privately by J. Ridgway, 1839.

The Dream and Other Poems. London: Henry Colburn, 1840.

The Child of the Islands. London: Chapman & Hall, 1845.

Fisher's Drawing-Room Scrap-Book. 1846-48.

Letters to the Mob. Published first in The Morning Chronicle: collected 1848.

Stuart of Dunleath. A Novel 1851.

English Laws for Women in the Nineteenth Century. Printed for private circulation 1854.

A Letter to the Queen on Lord Cransworth's Marriage and Divorce Bill. London: Longman, Brown, Green & Longmans, 1855.

The Lady of La Garaye. A Poem. London: Macmillan, 1862.

Lost and Saved. A Novel. London: Hurst & Blackett, 1863.

Poems and Sketches in *Macmillan's Magazine* 1861-75.

Old Sir Douglas. 1875.

ENGLISH LAWS FOR WOMEN.

"It won't do to have Truth and Justice *on our side;*

We must have Law and Lawyers.*"**

CHARLES DICKENS

INTRODUCTION

I take those words as my text. In consequence of the imperfect state of law, I have suffered bitterly, and for a number of years: I have lately been insulted, defrauded, and libelled: and as the law is constituted, I find redress impossible.

To publish comments on my own case for the sake of obtaining sympathy; to prove merely that my husband has been unjust, and my fate a hard one, would be a very poor and barren ambition. I aspire to a different object. I desire to prove, not my suffering or his injustice, but that the present law of England cannot prevent any such suffering, or control any such injustice. I write in the hope that the law may be amended; and that those who are at present so ill-provided as to have only "Truth and Justice" on their side, may hereafter have the benefit of "Law and Lawyers."

* Bleak House, page 529.

1

I know all that can be said on my interference with such a subject; all the prejudice and contempt with which men will receive arguments from a woman, and a woman personally interested. But it is of more importance that the law should be altered, than that I should be approved. Many a woman may live to thank Heaven that I had courage and energy left, to attempt the task: and, since no one can foretell the future, even men may pause ere they fling down my pamphlet with masculine scorn; for a day may come,—however improbable—to some one of my readers, when he would give his right hand, for the sake of sister, daughter, or friend, that the law *were* in such a condition as to afford a chance of justice; without the pain of a protracted struggle, or the disgrace of a public brawl. What I write, is written in no spirit of rebellion; it puts forward no absurd claim of equality; it is simply an appeal for protection. Such protection, in degree, as is accorded to servants, to apprentices, to the sailor on the high seas, to all whom the law admits to be in a subordinate and helpless position. Such protection, in degree, as has lately been extended to women in the lower classes, by the more stringent laws enacted in their behalf.

In arguing my case from my own example, I am not ignorant that there are persons who think such argument blameable on other grounds; who deem a husband's right so indefeasible, and his title so sacred, that even a wronged wife should keep silence. How far will they carry that principle? A few years ago, a French nobleman, the Duc de Praslin, assassinated his wife in the midst of her slumbering household. When morning broke, she was dead; but many a proof remained of the desperate resistance, and agonized efforts to escape, made by that wretched woman before her doom was completed. Do the advocates of the doctrine of non-resistance consider that her duty would have been to submit tranquilly to the fate pre-determined for her? If not, let them waive judgment in my case; for if choice were allowed me, I would rather be murdered and remembered by friends and children with love and regret, than have the slanders believed which my husband has invented of me. It is he, who has made silence impossible. With *him* rests the breaking of those seals

2

which keep the history of each man's home sacred from indifferent eyes. He has declared himself my deadliest foe, whose dagger has too near an aim to miss my heart—and, of the two, I hold his stab to be worse than that of the Duc de Praslin, for he would assassinate even my memory.

I resist.

For the shallower rebuke, that mine is an exceptional case; that the law need scarcely be disturbed to meet a solitary instance of tyranny, there is a ready and reasonable answer. ALL cases requiring legal interference are exceptional cases; and it will scarcely be argued that a balance must first be struck in numbers, and instances of wrong be reckoned by the dozen or the gross, before justice will condescend to weigh the scales. But it does not follow that mine is a solitary example of injustice, because it may possibly happen, from a combination of peculiar circumstances, to be the instance which shall call attention to the state of the law. Hundreds of women are suffering at this moment, whose cases are not less hard, but more obscure: and it consists with all experience, that although wrong and oppression may be repeated till they become almost of daily occurence, they strike at last on some heart that revolts instead of enduring; or are witnessed by men who indignant sympathy works out reform and redress. In either case, oppression is brought to a halt, not by a multitude of instances, but by some single example; which example may be neither more nor less important than others, though it be made the argument and opportunity of change. We are not told that any extraordinary perfection marked for defence the peasant child of William Tell; nor Watt Tyler's daughter; nor even that virgin girl of Rome, for whom her sire chose death rather than degradation; the doom had fallen, perhaps, on other victims quite as worthy. But it was resisted for *them* by hearts that beat high in defence of honest right; and therefore (and not for the value of the victims) we read in the records of history, of a pagan father who took his child's life; of Christian fathers who perilled their own; and of those convulsions, changes, and tumults, which had their proximate and apparent cause in the desire to avenge a tyrannous act done to a peasant's son—to punish insult offered to a craftsman's daughter—to keep from defilement one weak girl, claimed by a despotic ruler, in the market-place of superb Rome—but whose root was in this established certainty; that in all human societies, great general injustice shall be checked, sooner or later, by individual resistance.

If, as I have said, it does not necessarily follow that the example of resistance is also the example of crowning wrong; so neither does it follow that there is tyranny greater than usual enacted, when the benefactor arises, whose chivalrous nature sees cause for exertion, where other men saw none. Not even then, in the merit of the sufferers, or the degree of their suffering, lies the prospect of change; but in the spirit of him who will not tamely contemplate any misery he thinks he might relieve. He follows in the track of those who have all *"passed by on the other side;"* but he differs from them in this, that he pauses to know what wounded and moaning thing is flung across his path, and forthwith accepts as his business, that task of rescue which more selfish and careless men have declined. The good Samaritan in Scripture addressed himself to no peculiar case; he lifted no bleeding hero from a disastrous battle-field; nor king writhing under the assassin's stroke. A man lay groaning who had fallen among thieves. That is all we shall ever know of the example of help, given as a lesson of charity eighteen hundred years ago, to the fleeting generations of the world!

In these later days of more complicated social wrong; when HOWARD rose amongst us; apostle of compassion to sufferers barred out of sight; our prisons were no worse than they had been, nor our prisoners better men; their dungeons were not darker, nor their food more scant, nor their sighing louder, nor their case more pitiful, than theirs who had gone before. Circumstance was the same, but the hazard of help had arrived. The sighing was heard, the darkness was perceived, the hunger for human pity was satisfied, not for the sake of those especial prisoners, but because HOWARD was come. So in ERSKINE's time; the laws were not more oppressive, nor their operation more unequal, than in a generation foregone; nor were the men who had to abide by the legal

4

decisions of the day, unusually notable and important. They were the common clients of common causes, suffering under common and established grievances, arising from those defects in our patched-up system, which no one yet had cared to examine, or had found sufficient energy to correct. But ERSKINE came; and when men told him that such defects were part of the law "before he was born," he answered, that it was "because he was not born, that it was law," for that he would see it altered before he died.

So with ROMILLY: it was no new thing that roused his earnest nature to struggle for reforms in the science of that profession which he at once adorned and detested. Many a prisoner without counsel, had stood wistfully at the bar before ROMILLY's time; listening to learned accusations dimly understood, destitute of defence. Many a long-standing blur and blot lay unremoved on the great scroll of our national code; when his warm eloquence, enlarged views, profound thought, and keen comparison with the universal law of nations, worked together for its amendment. He did not plead (for he could not so have pleaded) that the men of his day who found no help from that code, were peculiar martyrs; of higher desert, with more atrocious injuries to redress, and with less chance of redressing them, than heretofore. He knew that this was not the case. All was common, usual, inevitable; and because being common, usual, and inevitable, it was also *unjust*, and not for merit in the sufferers, or excess in any one case of suffering, he strove for change, and effected it.

We need the heart of a ROMILLY amongst us now. That strenuous heart, whose energetic pity made no compromise with custom; nor ever flagged or fainted in the life-long effort to serve his fellow-men, till, in an hour of delirious regret, its strong pulse was stilled for ever.*

If *he* were here—if he were here, who so valued the wedded companion of his own home, that when she died he

---

* Sir Samuel Romilly lost his wife, after a long and happy union, on the 29th October, 1818. After four days and nights of excessive anguish and grieving, his mind became disturbed, and he committed self-destruction.

sank, scathed by her loss as by lightning—he would not answer with contented apathy, "*It is the law*," when women complain of injustice! He would stand for the right now, as he stood in those other days, when he nobly strove, and patiently planned, to make Law what it should be, a means of protection, not an engine of oppression, to the weak. Is there no one with heart great enough to fill his place?

It is the law. Can anything be more curious than the crabbed obstinacy or despairing sight with which this reply is made? as though we had for our guidance the edicts of the Medes and Persians, of which it was fabled that they involved no principle of change. Yet changes are perpetually made in the most stringent edicts we have. That which was law to the generation of yesterday, is not law to us; and that which is law to us, may be reversed for the generation of tomorrow; why should unjust laws for women be more permanent than other unjust laws? We know that LAW was mapped and planned among civilised nations as the great Highway to JUSTICE. Where the road leads astray, it should be mended or altered: and it is one of the boasts of our ever-boastful England, that she does this. Not indeed of a sudden, with the stroke of some magic wand; but after fitful struggle and delay, as all things are done on this travailing earth; a delay proportioned to the strength of ancient prejudices, the jealousy of contending interests, the energy or slackness of the hands that do the work.

Neither my space—nor my bounded knowledge—will permit that I should follow, in detail, even the most recent of those changes; but take such instance as the hazard of memory, or the very shallowest chance-reference can supply; take them entirely from among facts within the cognizance of living men; and you shall crowd into a few pages, such reversal of mercantile, political, social, and religious rights, as have altered the destinies of the entire population of England. Our children are born to the tranquil inheritance of privileges that were struggled for in our time, with fury, ferment, and heart-break. They stand on conquered ground; ground that was inch by inch a battle-field to their fathers. They exchange among themselves as current and common

6

coin, those treasures of Liberty that freighted our argosies in stormier days; when they who watched the doubtful chance, knew not if they should witness the sinking of the wreck, or cheer our entrance to the haven. Some of the captains of those days are at rest; but some are yet among us; witnesses of the folly of those who would set a changeless limit to that which of all things is most susceptible of change in the onward progress of a nation—the code by which its social interests are governed.

Where is the great question of Roman Catholic Emancipations? Where are the restrictions on trade? The first, already seems to our children almost a matter of History; yet there are living men who heard CANNING give BROUGHAM the lie direct in the English Senate, when that question trembled in the balance, and the brilliant Advocate of many causes, in the keen anxiety of the hour, taunted the new Minister with exchanging for the triumphs of office the support he had previously afforded it. The other is a change of yesterday. Fresh, in the mourning memory of his friends, is the death of that leader who moored the vessel of the State in an untried anchorage, with the scornful words that he refused to direct its course *"by observations taken in 1842,"* and that he would feel less humiliated by the charge of inconsistency, than by any supposed fear of acknowledging that he had altered his opinions.

Whether it be contended that our rulers were enlightened or struck blind when they projected such changes—the changes were made: every portion of those two systems remains for our children, a law reversed or a barrier broken down.

Where are the grosser corruptions of our Parliamentary representation? Swept away one morning in a storm of cheers. Yet it is not so long since Lord John Russell attempted to sow the first fragile seed of the Reform Bill, by proposing that rotten boroughs should be purchased by the nation; their owners to receive compensation from an indebted country, for the extinguished right of selling shares in what is supposed to be the aggregate Voice of the People. It is not so long since the same Minister of Liberty urged the claim of those great

7

capitals of mercantile interest, Manchester, Birmingham, and Leeds, to be represented in the lower house, and urged that claim in vain: since he complained of national apathy on the subject which afterwards shook England to its centre; and beheld that great measure of Reform which, like the burden of Sisyphus, he had heaved up so often only to see it roll back to its former position—allowed at length to rest in the English Senate—by favour of a majority of ONE.

These are changes, affecting political rights; struggled for by political men; opposed or upheld by the whole mass of the people: but there are others, affecting sections of the community, in which an equal or even greater amount of alteration has been effected, and in which the value and power of individual effort is more distantly visible. Our Schools, our Prisons, and our Mad-houses, are all under Government supervision. Their occupants form classes set apart—by helplessness of age, by error of conduct, and by the visitation of God—from those that have free control of their destiny; and we point with pride to the model regularity of system and of architecture which we have recently introduced for the better management of their interests. How was it before the change could be effected? How was it, first, with the most miserable of those classes, the insane? Obscure struggles, half measures, renewed efforts, mark the progress from 1763 till, in the year 1788, Mason the Poet wrote a pamphlet, finding bitter fault with the management of the York Asylum. The tone of his pamphlet was condemned. There is nothing society resents so much, as having the duckweed on the still pond of its surface disturbed by the under-current of struggling lives. Society did not want to hear about such horrors; society was of opinion they could not be helped. Mr. Mason was loudly blamed for his interference; and he and his pamphlet were thrust aside. About three years afterwards, the relatives of an insane Quaker being discontented with the regulations of the same Asylum, renewed the complaints Mason had made; and followed them up with considerable perseverance. Little was done, however, except that the "Retreat" at York was established by the Quakers themselves. Every sort of obstacle was thrown in the way of public

8

inquiry. At length (with praiseworthy ingenuity), thirteen gentleman qualified as Governors of the York Asylum by paying twenty guineas each, for the express purpose of getting a committee of the House of Commons appointed to examine into this matter. They did get the Committee appointed; the expenses of most of the witnesses being paid by a subscription raised among the ladies of York; and thus began that interference with a monstrous evil, which is now a matter of regular government control. In the particular instance of the York Asylum, the most horrible abuses were discovered. There were but two servants to one hundred and twenty male patients; the funds had been misapplied; the books and registers burned; the grossest immorality practised; and in the report of deaths, 144 out of 365 had been suppressed. As the inquiry spread to other asylums, more and more horrors were made known. When Mr. Wakefield visited Bethlem, among countless other instances of cruelty one man was found with an iron ring round his neck, an iron bar round his waist, and iron pinions on his arms, fastened to the wall; and this had endured twelve years at the pleasure of one of the keepers. In the House of Correction at Kendal a man had been in solitary confinement ten years, though he had intervals of sanity of nine and ten months' duration. As to the condition of insane women, it was one to shudder at, not to speak of. In private mad-houses (in spite of an act passed in 1774*) matters were as bad, or worse; and one of the visiting physicians declared he was ill with the atmosphere of their filth, "although accustomed to the dissecting-room." At length, in 1816 a bill passed the Commons (and was lost in the Lords) "for the better Regulation of Mad-houses;" and gradually that came to be a public and redressed wrong, which had been an obscure grievance.

Of our prison discipline, much the same history may be told. Long after Howard's time (who declared in 1773, that so miserably off were these kennelled sufferers, that "to rot in jail," was an exact and not a figurative expression, and that more persons perished thus, than by public execution), our

---

* Brought under the notice of Parliament ten years previously.

prisons remained, for the most part, dens of corruption, disease and torture. In 1804, Mr Neild, a magistrate of Aylesbury, (Secretary to a Society for the relief and discharge of poor Debtors), published, in the "Gentleman's Magazine," observations on Chelmsford and Colchester Bridewells. He afterwards published an account of all the jails in this island; which he had visited unauthorised and unaided, Government doing nothing to help him in his self-imposed task; and obstacles having been thrown in his way which would have wearied out any less benevolent patience. From 1804 to 1812, he appears to have been ceaseless in his endeavours to procure some amendment; and though, when Fowell Buxton followed in 1818, and when Mrs Fry devoted herself to the female prisoners of Newgate, very little general improvement was perceptible; yet much was done in Neild's time to make progress almost certain, and a retrograde movement impossible. The jail of Aylesbury (with whom he was more immediately connected), and other prisons, controlled in their management by men like himself, became what it is the cant term of the day to call "Model Prisons." The abuses of those he could not control, were exposed by him. It became *known* that in the Borough Compter prison the debtors lay upon boards; in filth, damp, and discomfort; felons and debtors all huddled together; no classification, no comfort, no decency. That in Ayr jail, the prisoners lay on straw, till Mr Neild supplied blankets from his own private charity. That in Edinburgh jail, the same miseries and even greater were endured; no employment was permitted; and felons (with an enlightened regard for the state of their souls) were absolutely excluded by rule, *from attendance on divine service.* In the privileged prison of Dover Castle, when its warder was the great Minister Lord Liverpool (who had been preceded by Mr Pitt), the prison-fees were so enormous that prisoners might remain twenty months in the Castle *at the suit of the Crown*, for sums totally irrespective of the real debt for which they were incarcerated. The prison was in a state of shameful dilapidation; and a Quaker gentleman gave 800*l.* in the three per cents, to pave the courtyard of this royal jail, and make permanent provision to aid the poorer debtors in obtaining their release. These were merely samples of the condition of most of the prisons in Great Britain. In Fowell Buxton's time the Borough Compter was little altered; dirt, confusion, and misery; cold, sickness, and gambling; and twenty prisoners sleeping on eight straw beds. This, again, a mere sample of the condition of other jails. In Mrs Fry's time, Newgate, which was built to hold 480, held from 800 to 1200; no classification, no employment, no instruction; filth that sickened and turned the heart faint; instances of debtors actually starving in jail; the accused and convicted, sick and well, abandoned women, and children young enough to be in the nursery, all huddled together; prisoners employed in gambling, and complaining that they had nothing else to do. Idleness, contamination, riot, sickness and blasphemy; no rest by night, and no peace by day; only corruption, mental and physical, hourly leavening among neglected swarms of fellow-creatures, with bodies to care for and souls to be saved.

To the efforts, first of one earnest individual, and then of another, must be attributed the attention slowly granted by successive Governments to these great abuses; until at length the greater part of our prisons have become a triumph and a show; from the regulations of which it needs only that some future Neild should expunge the barbarous mistake of prolonged solitary confinement, to make them as perfect as places of the kind can be.

To the efforts of earnest individuals, must also be attributed that control now exercised over the education of the poor. Where was England in this respect fifty or sixty years since? In 1798, a Mr Lancaster opened a school in the Borough road, which in seven years became a free school for one thousand children. The expenses of Mr Lancaster's plan outran his means; and a Mr Joseph Fox gave bills for 3,600l. to take the school out of debt, risking this sum without any very clear prospect of repayment, for the sake of the cause. Other generous and public-spirited men then came forward, and Mr Lancaster travelled through the country giving lectures and explaining his scheme. In consequence of those lectures, forty five schools, educating 11,300 children were estab-

11

lished; in the year 1809, fifty schools, educating 14,200 children, were organised; and at length, at a meeting held at the Freemason's Tavern on the 11th of May, 1811—two Royal Princes (the Duke of York and the Duke of Sussex), moved and seconded a resolution, that Mr Lancaster deserved the thanks and support of all England, for that in four years he had been the means of causing 25,000 children to be educated; and Mr Francis Horner at the same meeting declared, that of the 7,000 children educated in Lancaster's own school in the Borough road, not one had ever been charged in a court of justice with any criminal offence.

With the great educational movement which afterwards took place, and the endeavour to make the state in some degree responsible for the training of the people, Lord BROUGHAM's name must for ever be nobly associated. With him (one of the most scientifically educated men of his day), rested the task of arguing away the absurd prejudice, that if the lower classes were instructed, they would disdain to work; with him rested the long struggle against the abuses of charitable trusts, and bequests for educational purposes; the sacredness of which was so little understood, that Lord Kenyon remarked of the grammar schools, that *"everything was neglected except the receipt of salaries and emoluments;"* and Lord Eldon, that *"all over the Kingdom, charity estates were dealt with in a manner amounting to the most direct breach of Trust."* There was no such tranquil admission on all sides as exists to-day, that the State is bound to watch over and secure to its poorer millions the inestimable blessing of education. Lord Brougham was flouted and opposed; and in nothing did he encounter more opposition or greater odium, than in his attempt to prevent this embezzlement of the property of the poor. With most pertinacious energy he made himself their pioneer to knowledge; and most assuredly, when the balance of usefulness is struck in his dazzling and eccentric career, the triumph can never be denied him of having been a main means of securing to future generations of Englishmen, the first of life's blessings both in date and degree; that early and orderly training which lifts a toiling man above the level of a toiling brute; which teaches

12

him to use the powers of his soul in addition to the powers of the body; which makes slumber and food no longer the sole refreshment of the intelligent artisan, and throws a light into the labourer's cottage beyond the common light of day.

It is not because I undervalue the help thus given at a later stage of the cause, that I endeavoured to mark the moment when national progress was set on foot by individual energy.* I know that when Lancaster's theory was made public, the Duke of Bedford and Lord Somerville became eager supporters of his scheme; that the King and all the Royal Family warmly assisted him (as they afterwards did his some-time rival, Dr Bell); and that in process of time, the liberality of the public became so general, that the Lancastrian schools seemed supported rather by the levying of a national tribute, than by the payment of collected subscriptions. But that which I insist upon, is the small beginning from which these great results were evolved. Not by national acclamation of an all-pervading plan, but by the resolute and

---

* In 1787—that which Mr Lancaster achieved many years afterwards for ENGLAND, was attempted for IRELAND by Mr Thomas Sheridan, son of Dr Sheridan (the friend of Swift), and the father of R.B. Sheridan. Though not a scholar by profession—as Dr Sheridan was—he had great classical attainments, and the degree of Master of Arts was conferred on him both at Oxford and Cambridge. He wrote much on practical education; the necessity of learning "common things;" and the folly of confining instruction so much to the study of the dead languages. He had long planned a National Establishment for Ireland; funds for which he believed might in the first instance be raised, by putting down free schools where, from gradual abuse, no duty was done. When his two sons, Charles and Richard Brinsley, were in conspicuous public situations—Charles as Secretary-of-War in Ireland, and the younger, and more distinguished, in the zenith of his fame in England— Mr T. Sheridan reckoned on obtaining the notice and support of Government for his educational schemes, more especially as Mr Orde (Secretary to the Duke of Rutland), took an eager interest in them. The death, however, of the Duke, and the removal of Mr Orde, checked his projects; nor was it likely he would at that time obtain much encouragement. The then Ministry was far too busy with the intrigues of a divided Court—the impeachment of the Governor-General of India—the payment of the Crown Prince's debts—and the disputes whether Fox had or had not mocked the English Senate with a deliberate falsehood, sealed with that Prince's word, relative to the marriage with Mrs Fitzherbert—to have time to spare for a sanguine Irishman's plans for educating his countrymen; and in the ensuing year Mr Sheridan died.

13

patient struggle of a private individual—that great scheme of National Instruction was begun! When it appeared likely to fail for want of funds, a private individual (Mr JOSEPH Fox), risked his 3,600*l.* to save it from evil chance. To him joined five other private gentlemen (Mr JACKSON, Mr ALLEN, Mr CORSTON, Mr STURGE, and Mr FOSTER, who subscribed and obtained subscriptions from others, and formed themselves into a committee to manage Mr Lancaster's affairs. When that brilliant meeting of the 11th of May 1811, was held, it was rather to applaud what had been achieved, than to rouse to action: to congratulate on foregone victories; and to obtain fresh subsidies for the successful general who had carried on the battle against ignorance with an army of volunteers. Before those Royal Princes the Duke of KENT and Duke of SUSSEX,—or the Chancellor of the Prince Regent,—or the Duke of BEDFORD, Marquis of LANSDOWNE, Lord KEITH, FRANCIS HORNER, and HENRY BROUGHAM,—proposed resolutions at the Freemason's Tavern as "Friends of the Royal Lancasterian System for the Education of the Poor,"—Mr LANCASTER had laboured in his vocation *for thirteen years.* When his school was first opened in the Borough road, probably his very name was unknown to most of these great personages, and many a name, less notable and less remembered, had given substantial aid to the cause, before they became its patrons.

And now let me ask,—is there any reason why attention should not be called to the defective state of Laws for Women in England, as attention has been called to other subjects;—namely, by individual effort? Is there any reason why (attention being so called to the subject) Women alone, of the more helpless classes,—the classes set apart as not having free control of their own destinies,—should be denied the protection which in other cases supplies and balances such absence of free control? Are we to believe that the gentlemen of Great Britain are so jealous of their privilege of irresponsible power in this one respect, that they would rather know redress *impossible* in cases which they themselves admit to be instances of the grossest cruelty and baseness, than frame laws of control for themselves, such as they are willing to frame for others? Will they eagerly restrict the labourer or mechanic from violence and brutality in his wretched home, and yet insist on their own right of ill-usage as a luxury fairly belonging (like the possibility of divorce) to the superior and wealthy classes? Is there,—in the disposition of those who are to legislate,—an insurmountable barrier to fair legislation on this subject? and if not, is there any reason why (to plead the cause of the inferior sex as humbly as possible) the laws and enactments for their protection should not undergo as much revision, with as fair a chance of beneficial alteration, as the regulations affecting the management of pauper children,—insane patients,—and the tried and untried prisoners who occupy our goals?

I forget; I might plead yet more humbly; I might drop yet one great step in the social scale, to find a more exact parallel with the legal position of women in this country.

England has lately made a sort of ovation to an American lady, whose graphic and impassioned appeal on the anti-slavery question, reached Europe in the guise of a romance; a romance which has since been translated into most modern languages,—so that "Uncle Tom's Cabin" has become everywhere a "household word." Had I been in England at the time Mrs Beecher Stowe visited us, I too, would have considered it a privilege and joy to see one whose genius glorified that solemn and gloomy argument, and sent it amongst us clothed in light. I wish her success. I desire heartily for her that her name may hereafter be remembered with a blessing, among the names of those who were early labourers in a day now dawning, that shall bring help to the helpless. I hold her task to be a holy one, and slavery an accursed thing.

But, meanwhile, it may not be uninteresting to those Americans who are of a contrary opinion, and who have felt wounded at the manner in which we have called across the Atlantic to bid America renounce the error of her way,—to look back to the time,—when so new and unwelcome was our conversion to the creed of mercy, in our own colonies, that Lord Seaforth wrote home to Ministers in 1802, to say he had offended the whole island of Barbadoes by endeavouring to persuade them that the wilful murder of a slave should

15

be made felony, instead of being compounded for by a fine of 11*l.* 4*s.* The time when Wᴵᴸᴮᴇʀꜰᴏʀᴄᴇ was a struggling enthusiast in an uncertain cause; when our King, Prince of Wales, and the whole of the Royal Family (with the single exception of the Duke of Gloucester), were opposed to the Abolition Bill; when Pitt despaired of carrying that measure, and it was a hot angry war among Englishmen whether it should pass or not. A war which continued through years of debating and pamphleteering, before the victory was won by our Abolitionists.

It may not be uninteresting to Americans to know, also, that if they will examine the reports of our House of Commons,—after that struggle was fairly ended, and the new law had been passed,—they will find the prototype of "Lᴇɢʀᴇᴇ" in the person of "Aʀᴛʜᴜʀ Hᴏᴅɢᴇ, Esq., one of the Members of his Majesty's Council for the Virgin Islands,"—who, in the year 1811, was brought to trial and condemned for the murder of a slave named Prosper on his estate in the island of Tortola,—when his countless cruelties were exposed, in sworn depositions preserved in those records. There, Americans may find the original of Uɴᴄʟᴇ Tᴏᴍ, in "Tᴏᴍ Bᴏɪʟᴇʀ, a stout, hale, hearty man," who, in the year 1807, was laid down and flogged without intermission for more than an hour by order of Hᴏᴅɢᴇ, and being unable to rise after the flogging, was carried to the sick-house; lingered a few days; and then died. There, they will find it computed that sixty of Hodge's slaves had perished in three years from severity of punishment, and not more than three, in that period, had died a natural death. About a dozen of these wretched victims are named in the affidavits reported to our house of Commons; among whom are women and children: one child of ten years old, named Tᴀᴍsᴇɴ, having been dipped (*by order*) into a copper of boiling liquor, and two of the women having had boiling water poured down their throats. Yet when this subject of King George of England was tried, it was pleaded for him in open court that a negro being property, it was no greater offence in law for his owner to kill him than to kill a dog: the jury, though they returned a verdict of "guilty," by a majority of their number, recommended Hodge to mercy:

16

and Governor Elliott wrote home in his despatches, that he was obliged to be present, as Commander-in-chief,—to call out the militia,—and to proclaim martial law,—in order to secure the execution of the sentence. It is a remarkable additional fact, and shows the state of feeling at that time, that although these and a thousand other horrors were perfectly well known, ARTHUR HODGE, Esq., was well received in the society of the island, and retained his rank as "one of the Members of his Majesty's Council" up to the day of his arrest.

But these are things of the past: horrible shadows, remembered like bad dreams: events that never can occur again where England's law has sway. For England is just and merciful; and if she is also a little proud and preaching, it is no more than all converts to good causes are apt to be, in the fresh earnestness of their desire that truths lately brought home to themselves, should be brought home to others; and if she finds fault with the laws that permit oppression in the code of other countries, it is that she has no law which permits oppression in her own.

I beg the attention of both my American and English readers to a case I find copied, from a report in a "Cincinnati Gazette," into the columns of our own "Times" newspaper, in the month of November, 1853. It was a case tried in the Covington Circuit Court; and by the report it appears, that a slave named Sam Norris, belonging to a Mr J.N. Patton, of Virginia, had been permitted to work in Covington, on condition of paying each year a certain sum to his master; which sum was accordingly paid: that two years ago, Mr Patton proposed that the slave should purchase his freedom by the payment of a certain additional sum, which sum was nearly paid up when Mr Patton changed his mind, rescinded the contract, and claimed Sam Norris as his slave. The case was argued with much ability; but at the close of the argument the judge decided for Mr Patton against Sam Norris, on this principle, that by the law of Kentucky, "*a slave cannot make a contract, nor can he have monies of his own.*" The contract, therefore, was null and void; and the money, though received and expended by the master, could not be held *legally* to have been paid. The report concludes with this consolatory

17

admission, that the Hon. Judge Pryor, before whom the case was tried, "characterised it as one of great hardship and cruelty; and every one in the court-room seemed to sympathise deeply with the poor negro." In that sympathy I most truly share; but the case has besides a peculiar interest for me,—inasmuch as I find, in the slave law of Kentucky, an exact parallel of the law of England for its married women; and in this passage in the life of the poor slave Sam Norris, an exact counterpart of what has lately occurred in my own.

I, too, had a contract. My husband being desirous to raise money settled on me and my sons, to employ on his separate estate, and requiring my consent in writing before that could be done, gave me in exchange for such consent a written contract drawn up by a lawyer, and signed by that lawyer and himself. When he had obtained and employed the money he was desirous to raise, like Mr Patton of Virginia he resolved to *"rescind the contract."* When I, like the slave Norris, endeavoured to struggle against this gross breach of faith,—I was informed that by the law of England, *"a married woman could not make a contract, or have monies of her own."* When I complained of it,—I was punished by a flood of libellous accusations, published in all the English newspapers; libels for which, though *proved* falsehoods, I could obtain no redress, because they were published by my husband. The circumstance that Mr Norton, like Mr Patton, had obtained all the advantage he sought when he went through the formality and pretence of making a contract with me, made no difference; and as to money, even that which I earned by literature was subject to the claim of my husband, as the manual labor of the slave was subject to the claim of his master,—because a married woman is, by the code of England (as Sam Norris by the code of Kentucky), *non-existent* in law. It is fit that I should add, in behalf of English hearts and English love of justice, that when I stood, with that vain contract in my hand, in the Westminster County Court (I, an intelligent educated woman, granddaughter of a man sufficiently distinguished to have obtained sepulture in Westminster Abbey, hard by), and when the law was shown to be, for me, what it is for the slave in Kentucky, there was, in the

18

court-room of the Westminster County Court, as there was in the court-room of the Covington Circuit Court, evidence of strong sympathy. My case—which opened up a history of wrong, treachery, libel, and injustice endured for years without redress—was evidently considered like that of Norris, to be "one of great hardship and cruelty," and the concluding words with which Mr Norton vehemently attempted to address the court, were drowned in the groans and hooting of an excited crowd. But sympathy could do no more for me than for Mr Patton's slave. It could not force open for me the iron gates of the *Law* which barred out justice. It could not prevent libel, and torment, and fraud; the ripping up of old wounds, or the infliction of new. The *Law* alone could do that, if fit laws of protection existed for women. That they do not exist, is my complaint.

That they do not exist, might point a scornful answer from nations we imperiously lecture on the internal economy of their own governments. We have rebuked America, taunted Naples, complained of Sweden, remonstrated with Tuscany, condemned Portugal, and positively shuddered at Austria (in the person of Haynau), because slavery in the one, the treatment of political prisoners in another, religious intolerance in a third, and, above all, the treatment of WOMEN in the last, offends our very souls. Is England then incapable of any but a BORRIOBODS mission? Is she for ever to prefer making a sort of "Sterne's Sentimental Journey" into other countries, to fulfilling her duties at home? The foreigners we are so fond of reproving, see with disgust and abhorrence our own method of dealing with certain laws. To them, our mercantile and uncertain speculation of "damages,"—the wonderful indecency of our divorce trials,—the incredible fact that the woman accused is allowed no direct defence, and cannot appear by counsel on such occasions—the loth and reluctant admission (and that of very recent date) of the right of a mother to her infant children,—are alike odious and incomprehensible. I will venture to say that in no country in Europe, is there, *in fact*, so little protection of women as in England. England the fault-finder; England the universal lecturer; England—where to add to the absurd anomaly of

19

this state of things, the Salique law is considered a barbarism, and offence against a female Sovereign is treason. The contrast between that which we permit, and that which we disallow, borders almost on the burlesque. If Mr Norton, a magistrate and member of the aristocracy, had cheated at a game of cards played by a few idlers in one of the clubs of London, all England would have been in a ferment. Accusers would have risen; friends would have hung their heads; and for the sake of some dandy's purse, the invocation to justice would have been made in such a stern universal shout, as would have sent an echo all through Europe. Of if I, while visiting foreign lands, had invested myself with the dignity of a self-appointed messenger of God; if I had broken down the fence that guards other men's consciences, and trespassed there to sow what I considered "the good seed;" if I had forced on reluctant Roman Catholics, tracts of instruction in my own form of faith, and had been arrested for that trespass,—then indeed, I might hope to attract the attention of the Government of my own country, and my case might be warmly advocated at some such meeting as stood advertised in the English newspapers for Nov. 29, 1853, headed, "Persecuting Laws in Portugal, Tuscany, and Malta; the Earl of Shaftesbury in the chair." But in the English laws which wreck a woman's whole destiny; in the law which permits the most indecent and atrocious libel against her, without a chance of legal defence,—in the law which countenances and upholds far worse than cheating at cards, and renders null and void a contract signed by a magistrate, because that contract was made *with his wife*,—in the law which gives a woman's earnings even by literary copyright, to her husband,—in the whole framework, in short, of those laws by which her existence is merged in the existence of another (*let what will be the circumstances of her case*); and by which Justice in fact divests herself of all control and responsibility in the matter—England sees nothing worthy of remark.

With what a scornful retort might the nations we undertake to lecture, answer our busy-body meddling! "Protect your own women. Look at home for instances of tyranny, persecution, and unavailing appeals for justice. Do not trouble yourselves yet, about the denial of social rights to slaves, or those laws of Kentucky which seem in such harmony with your own; do not even pretend to shudder at the disgraceful chastisement inflicted on Austrian women, for what in their land is treason. Come to us when your magistrates do not make a profit of the law they administer; when your aristocracy are not guilty of violence and brutality to their wives, which they excuse by libels in your gazettes; when the daughters of your statesmen do not stand in your courts of law, ignobly baited for asserting just claims. That such things should occur, in your vain-glorious land, may be only a private and individual wrong; but that such things should occur, *with impunity*,—uncontrolled and unpunished by law,—is no longer a private wrong, but a national disgrace."

I shall now give a narrative of my own case, as an example of what can be done under the English law of 1853. If the publication fail to draw any permanent attention to the law itself, at least it will remain a curious record of injustice, in a country especially boastful of its liberal and magnanimous enactments. If the record appear unimportant as the mere history of a woman's wrongs, it may have interest as involving a passage in the life of one of England's Prime Ministers.

I have endeavoured to make the narrative as clear as possible, by dividing into three outlines,—1st, the strange mutual position of Mr Norton and myself with respect to money matters, both before and after our separation,—2dly, the treatment I received as a wife; taken from the papers submitted at the time to lawyers employed for me—and,—3dly, Lord Melbourne's opinion of the affairs in which his name was involved; copied word for word from his own letters. I have taken counsel of no one; and no one is responsible for the mention of names, or of the part taken by friends in these miserable affairs. If any see cause to regret what I have done, let them blame the *Law*. This pamphlet addresses itself, not to private sympathy, but to English justice: it is an attempt to argue the reform which ought to be, from the abuse that has been:—a complaint of the exercise of irresponsible power, to the source of power:—an appeal from THE LAW, as it stands, to the Legislature which frames and alters law.

I

I begin by an explanation of our mutual position as to money-matters; because Mr Norton has brought our disputes to a crisis on a pecuniary claim; because he has falsified the whole history of those matters; and because, from the first, our position in this respect was extraordinary and anomalous; inasmuch as instead of Mr Norton being, either by the exercise of his profession or patrimonial property, what Germans call the "Breadfinder," it was on my literary talents and the interest of my family, that our support almost entirely depended, while I still had a home.

Mr Norton has lately spoken (in the fabulous histories he has given to the public through the medium of the newspapers) of the profound and patient attachment he entertained for me previous to our union. I do most solemnly declare that at the time he first demanded me of my mother in marriage, I had not exchanged six sentences with him on any subject whatever. Mr Norton was brother to Lord Grantley; and the governess to whose care I was confided, happening to be sister to Lord Grantley's agent, the female members of the Norton family, from courtesy to this lady, invited her and such of her pupils as she chose to accompany her, to Lord Grantley's house.

A sister of Mr Norton's, an eccentric person who affected masculine habits and played a little on the violin, amused herself with my early verses and my love of music, and took more notice of me than of my companions. The occasions on which I saw this lady were not frequent; and still more rare were the occasions on which I had also seen her brother; it

23

was therefore with a feeling of mere astonishment, that I received from my governess the intelligence that she thought it right to refuse me the indulgence of accompanying her again to Lord Grantley's till she had heard from my mother; as Mr Norton had professed his intention of asking me in marriage. This lady is still living, and can answer for the exact truth of my statement.

Almost the first step Mr Norton took, after he had made my mother's acquaintance, was to beg her interest with a member of the royal family, whose good work with the Chancellor Eldon was to procure him a small legal appointment; and from the day we were married, he never ceased impressing upon me, that as I brought him no present fortune (my portion being only payable on my mother's death) I was bound to use every effort with the political friends of my grandfather, to get him lucrative promotion in his profession. I found this more difficult than I expected. The memory of Mr Sheridan among the Whig party, was not held in that affection which in my inexperience I had fancied; and if it had been, I do not know that it would have been a sufficient plea for serving Mr Norton, who could put forward no personal claims for employment. I did, however, what my husband requested.

I besieged, with variously worded letters of importunity, the friends whom I knew as the great names linked with the career of my grandfather; and while waiting the result of the petitions I had sown on so wide a field, I turned my literary ability to account, by selling the copyright of my first poem to Messrs. Ebers of Bond street. It is not without a certain degree of romantic pride that I look back, and know, that the first expenses of my son's life were defrayed from the price of that first creation of my brain; and before that child was two years old, I had procured for my husband,—(for the husband who has lately overwhelmed me, my sons, and his dead patron with slander, rather than yield a miserable annuity)—a place worth a thousand a year; the arduous duty of which consisted in attending three days in the week, for five hours, to hear causes tried in the simplest forms of law.

From that day to the present, my husband has always

considered that I ought to assist *him*—instead of his supporting *me*. The dependance upon my literary efforts for all extra resources, runs, as a matter of course, through all the letters I received from him during our union. The names of my publishers occur as if they were Mr Norton's bankers. If Murray of Albemarle street will not accept a poem,—if Bull of Holles street does not continue a magazine,—if Heath does not offer the editorship of an Annual,—if Saunders and Otley do not buy the MS. of a novel,—if Colburn's agreement is not satisfactory and sufficient,—if Power delays payment for a set of ballads,—if, in short, the *wife* has no earnings to produce, the *husband* professes himself to be "quite at a loss to know" how the next difficulty of payment is to be got over. On one occasion, when I had been employed to write words to Spanish music, by an officer of some distinction, and was extremely loth to express to this gentleman the opinion Mr Norton wished conveyed to him,—namely, that payment was too long delayed,—Mr Norton himself undertook the task of dunning him, for the stipulated sum by which *he* was to profit. I worked hard, and was proud of my success. I brought to my many tasks all the energy which youth, high spirits, ambition, good health, and the triumph of usefulness could inspire; joined to a wish for literary fame, so eager, that I sometimes look back and wonder if I was punished for it, by unenviable and additional notoriety.

I believe that foreigners,—and even our own mercantile classes,—have little idea of the very narrow provision which the usual "Right of the Eldest Son" leaves for the younger members of noble English houses. The rule is excellent, as a means of perpetuating a powerful and wealthy Aristocracy; the chief never being impoverished by that perpetual subdivision which takes place in other countries. But one result is, that the younger brothers and sons of Peers, (the habits of whose childhood and youth naturally were to enjoy an equality of luxury with the Heir,) are often embarrassed by the slenderness of their means: and this was our case. Luckily for me, light serial literature was the express fashion of the day. Nor did the greatest authors we had, disdain to contribute their share to the ephemeral "Annuals" and Periodicals, which formed the staple commodity of the booksellers at that time.

I rejoiced then, at finding,—woman though I was,—a career in which I could earn that which my husband's profession had never brought him. Out of our stormy quarrels I rose undiscouraged, and worked again to help him and forward the interests of my children. I have sat up all night,—even at times when I have had a young infant to nurse,—to finish tasks for some publisher. I made in one year a sum of 1,400*l.* by my pen; and I have a letter from Mr Norton's own brother, proving that even when we were on terms of estrangement, I still provided, without grudging, money that was to be spent on his pleasures.

As time went on, Mr Norton, still unsatisfied, urged upon me the task of obtaining for him, something more valuable than his magistracy, and of which the duties should be more agreeable. The petitioning recommenced; Lord Lyndhurst became Chancellor, and the hope of a legal appointment was again indulged. Nothing, however, was yet obtained; when a woman, to whose interference about my children our final quarrel was owing, began to rule entirely in my home. She has since left Mr Norton two thousand a year; and he openly entreated my patience with her, on account of her money. Lord Melbourne, for whose interest we had again applied, showed great reluctance to use it on Mr Norton's behalf; and had already expressed, in no measured terms, his regret at having made the former appointment. Undaunted by this fact, Mr Norton merely observed that if Lord Melbourne would not obtain a place, he could *privately* oblige him; and he applied accordingly to the patron he has lately reviled, for the loan of 1,500*l.*

Mr Norton considered that this loan was declined. Lord Melbourne told me that he merely demurred, as he doubted whether in reality it would be a *loan*. The condition of our affairs was not exactly known to me until that time; though the irritation arising from non-success was visited upon me. One of the bitter quarrels which blighted our home arose. Its record will be found with others; the present outline being confined to pecuniary matters. After that quarrel was made up, and I had returned to Mr Norton, he entered more fully upon a statement of his affairs; urging upon me most strenuously, to endeavour, as I had done before, to assist him, either by getting a more lucrative appointment or a loan of money. I expressed my astonishment that his own patrimonial resources never seemed to yield us anything; and received the information that there were no proceeds forthcoming from the hereditary estates. I doubted the correctness of this assertion; but wrote the very unwelcome intelligence, both to my mother and to one of the trustees of my marriage settlement. From my mother I received a letter containing the following passage:—

Hampton Court Palace.
Nothing could be more painful and surprising to me, than your statement of Norton's money-affairs. Had not D.K. vouched for the respectability of Mr P., and consequently for the fidelity of his statement of the property destined for the younger brothers and sisters of Lord Grantley, I never should have suffered you to marry N. He (Mr P) distinctly stated that property to be land, to the value of 30,000*l*., and if I get his direction from you, I will expostulate with him on the monstrous untruth then advanced; which may perhaps induce him, in his own vindication, to show how you have been cheated; which it is evident you have been. If Charles and James Norton join you, this affair might be cleared a little, and it is a manifest duty that you should exert yourself, for your poor *children*.

Exert myself, God knows I did; both to understand, and to avert, the mismanagement (or worse) that was taking place. The letter I addressed to my trustee, produced the following reply.

31st August, 1835.
As I was on the point of leaving London, Norton applied to me for my consent to raise a portion of the trust fund and to place the principal at his disposal. I told him I could do nothing of this kind without legal advice, and I could give no consent without the previous sanction of my solicitors. About a fortnight ago he applied to me to sign an order on Coutts and

27

Co. with reference to this same trust fund. I returned it unexecuted, to await the sanction of those in whose legal advice I could confide. Your statement of the present circumstances of the case, proves the precaution to have been necessary. As relates to Norton's power of raising money, he is clearly restrained by the terms of his own marriage settlement; and no personal debts of his, incurred subsequently to that settlement, can defeat rights which were vested by it; in other words, his CHILDREN have a better claim than his creditors to the principal sum secured under his marriage settlement.

I beg attention to the date of these letters; which were written but six months before our final separation, followed by the trial, attributed by Lord Melbourne (as will be seen in his correspondence) to another pecuniary endeavour on Mr Norton's part. I was already the mother of three children; and it must be confessed that our prospects were rendered discouraging by the extreme reluctance of powerful friends to do anything more for Mr Noton; and by the total and scornful alienation from him of all the male members of my family. I explained our position very fully to one of the kindest friends I had,—the Right Honourable Edward Ellice; and he drew out a paper of conditions, in which it was expressly stipulated that, if the difficulties in which Mr Norton found himself could be lightened, and any arrangement come to, our current income in future, and the whole management of our affairs, should be left in *my* hands; a stipulation significant enough as to Mr Norton's conduct in money-matters.

Our separation took place a few months after these discussions. Mr Norton did not at first speculate on divorcing me; he notified me that my family might support me, or that I might write for my bread; and that my children were by law at his sole disposal. Colonel Leicester Stanhope (now Earl of Harrington), who was commissioned, as a mutual friend, to announce this determination, appended to its following comment:—"N's proposal about your income is too bad, too shabby, too mean, too base; he grafts you on your brother." And the trustee I had previously consulted, observed:—"The propositions (which I return) are no less absurd than contemptible; and you could not hesitate one instant in rejecting them. They must think you have lost your brains, when they call on you to subsist by them, if they think you are fool enough to be gulled or bullied into such terms."

Mr Norton, however, soon proved what measures are at an English husband's disposal, whose wife demurs to any terms he chooses to impose. Those who saw their own advantage in our quarrel, advised him to make Lord Melbourne an object of attack; and under our mercantile law of "Damages," Mr Norton saw *his* advantage in adopting the suggestion. Lord Erskine, in one of his divorce cases, had obtained a verdict of 7000*l.*; (a sum which, in that particular case, was said to involve the whole fortune of the defendant) and Sir W. Follett did his best to emulate Lord Erskine, in urging this main object on the jury. He repeated in every form, his argument for aggravated compensation to his client. Sometime he put it as a simple and inevitable legal result,—*"If you are satisfied (as satisfied I think you must be, of the facts stated), it remains for you to consider what damages you will give."* Sometimes with a skilful and business-like allusion to the wealth which made a large sum a natural and proper award—"Of course," he says, "Of course, the position of the parties in this case, the rank of one of the parties, and the mode in which they lived being considered, it is for you, Gentlemen, under all circumstances, to say what may appear to you a proper amount of *damages.*" Sometimes, as an evidence of the wrong sustained, and the degree of that wrong,—"The amount of *damages,*—though not as a personal compensation,—must be considered in the result." Sometimes, as an appeal to the passions and sympathies of the jurymen; saying of Lord Melbourne—"His rank is an aggravation—his age is an aggravation—and the hollow pretence of his being a friend of the plaintiff, is a still greater aggravation. . . . It is then for you to say what *damages* you will give." Sometimes, with a sort of admonition to the jury to prove their own strictness of principle, by the amount of the penalty enforced,—"I call upon you to mark by your verdict,—in the only way in which the law allows,—your sense of the conduct of the defendant." Nothing was omitted to be urged that could be urged, on this point; and no doubt,—if the accusation had been believed,—very heavy damages would have been awarded; but the jury pronounced against Mr Norton, without even retiring to discuss their verdict, and the speculation failed; both as regarded political and pecuniary interests.

When the woman died, to whom my children had been sent, Mr Norton proposed to me to "forgive" the public trial, and return to him. After that, he proposed we should submit to referees; to whom he gave a written promise that he would abide by their decisions, and then refused to be bound. Then he advertised me as a run-away in the public papers; and he has, I believe, the unenviable distinction of being the only English gentleman who ever resorted to such an expedient; on which even my solicitor remarked: "There are few men in Mr Norton's rank of life, or in stations much under it, who will not know what to think of the measure." For two years I remained without one farthing of support from the husband who had owed to me the greater portion of his income. He then made what compulsory allowance he pleased; till in the year 1848, being desirous of employing the trust-fund settled on me and my children, in improving the estate left him by the woman to whom he first sacrificed us, he entered into the written contract with me, to which I have already alluded. The history of the breach of that contract will be found in my general narration, and I here close that portion which relates exclusively to pecuniary affairs.

II

The treatment I received as a Wife, would be incredible if, fortunately (or unfortunately), there were not witnesses who can prove it on oath. We had been married but a few weeks when I found that part of my lot was that which generally belongs to a lower sphere—and that, when angry, Mr Norton resorted to personal violence.

After our honeymoon, we lived for a short time in chambers Mr Norton had occupied as a bachelor, in Garden Court, Temple; and, on the first occasion of dispute, after some high and violent words, he flung the ink-stand, and most of the lawbooks, which might have served a better purpose, at the head of his bride. We had no servants there, but an old woman, who had taken care of these chambers for some years, and who offered me the acceptable consolation, that her master was not "sober,"—and would regret it "by-and-bye."

After this happy beginning, I accompanied my husband to Scotland. We had been married about two months, when, one evening, after we had all withdrawn to our apartments, we were discussing some opinion he had expressed; I said (very uncivilly), that "I thought I had never heard so silly or ridiculous a conclusion." This remark was punished by a sudden and violent kick; the blow reached my side; it caused great pain for many days, and being afraid to remain with him, I sat up the whole night in another apartment.

Four or five months afterwards, when we were settled in London, we had returned home from a ball; I had then no personal dispute with Mr Norton, but he indulged in bitter and coarse remarks respecting a young relative of mine, who, though married, continued to dance—a practice, Mr Norton said, no husband ought to permit. I defended the lady spoken

31

of, and then stood silently looking out of the window at the quiet light of dawn, by way of contrast. Mr Norton desired I would "cease my contemplations," and retire to rest, as he had already done; and this mandate producing no result, he suddenly sprang from the bed, seized me by the nape of the neck, and dashed me down on the floor. The sound of my fall awakened my sister and brother-in-law, who slept in a room below, and they ran up to my door. Mr Norton locked it, and stood over me, declaring no one should enter. I could not speak—I only moaned. My brother-in-law burst the door open, and carried me down stairs. I had a swelling on my head for many days afterwards, and the shock made my sister exceedingly ill.

On another occasion, when I was writing to my mother, Mr Norton (who was sipping spirits and water, while he smoked his cigar) said he was sure "from the expression of my countenance" that I was "complaining." I answered, that "I seldom could do anything else." Irritated by the reply, Mr Norton said I should not write at all, and tore the letter up. I took another sheet of paper, and recommenced. After watching and smoking for a few minutes, he rose, took one of the allumettes I had placed for his cigar, lit it, poured some of the spirits that stood by him over my writing book, and, in a moment, set the whole in a blaze. But Mr Norton vouchsafed no other notice of my alarm, than that it would "teach me not to brave him."

On another occasion, some time before the birth of my youngest son, I being at breakfast, and my eldest child playing about the room, Mr Norton entered; he desired me to rise and leave the place I was sitting in, as it faced the park, and it amused him to see the people pass by. I demurred, and said I was not well, and that he should have come down earlier if he had any fancy or choice about places. We had no other word of dispute. Mr Norton then deliberately took the tea-kettle, and set it down upon my hand; I started up from the pain, and was both burnt and scalded. I ran up to the nursery, and the nurse got the surgeon, who lived next door, to come in and dress my hand, which remained bound up and useless for days. When this was over, I enquired where Mr Norton was?

and received for reply, that after I had been hurt, he had simply desired the servant to "brush the crumbs away," in the place he had desired me to yield; had then sat down there and breakfasted; and had since gone out—without one word of apology or enquiry.]

About the same period, a dispute having arisen after dinner, I said I really was weary of my life with the perpetual wranglings; that I had a great deal to do, and would sit no longer with him, but go to the drawing-room and write for a Periodical of which I then had the editorship; that I only asked him to stay where he was, and smoke there, instead of upstairs. He answered that the house was his—not mine;— that he should sit in what room he pleased; and that I should find I could not carry things with such a high hand as I desired to do. I left him; called my maid, desired her to bring her work and remain in the room, as I did not feel well, and, locking the door of the drawing-room for further security, prepared to write. Mr Norton came and demanded admittance. I refused, and said I was undressing. After repeating his demand, and saying, if the door was not instantly opened he would break it open, he was as good as his word.

He forced in the door, forcing away the framework with it, and rushed forward. He stopped short on seeing my maid, and desired her instantly to leave the room. I said she must stay, for I was afraid of being left alone with him. Mr Norton then gave way to the most frantic rage, blew out the candles, flung the furniture about, and seized my maid to turn her out of the room by force. I clung to her, and being extremely frightened, and naturally at that time less strong than usual, I became very faint, and some of the other servants entering, Mr Norton desisted. He then lighted a taper, examined the door, asked where the carpenter lived, and left the room. I thought the worst was over; but I was mistaken.

Mr Norton returned almost immediately, and seizing me, forced me out of the room and down on the stairs. I really feared for my life; I shrieked for help, and said I was sure Mr Norton was "gone mad." The man-servant held back his arm while he was struggling with the maid, who was terrified to death—and at length, assisted by the servants, I retired once again to the nursery, and slept with the nurse; leaving Mr Norton master of the room he had broken into, and my literary tasks and the furniture scattered over the ground.

I intended to have left my home in the morning: but when morning came, I was too ill. I saw no more of Mr Norton till the evening of that day. I was sitting with my two little children in the same room. He did not speak to me—he spoke to one of the children and went away again. I had written to my brother to state all that had occurred. I said that for the sake of those children and the one unborn, I should be loth to part from my husband; that I bore him no ill-will, but that unless he would undertake to be "gentlemanlike" in his conduct towards me, I must leave him. My brother forwarded a copy of my statement to my husband,—told him there could be but one opinion of his cruel and violent assault, and that unless he received, within twenty-four hours, a written expression of contrition and promises for the future, he would expose Mr Norton.

To that letter I owe the miserable satisfaction of holding, under Mr Norton's own hand-writing, proof of every circumstance of this scene; for he undertook to justify himself to my brother; he admitted all the facts; he admitted that I had withdrawn to write for my publishers, and had told him so, but said he broke open the door "on principle; thinking it necessary, as a husband, to resist such extravagant and disrespectful proceedings" as locking him out of any room in the house. That he blew out the candles to prevent my maid remaining and working in the apartment; and that I had not seemed at all angry when I left him in the dining-room.

Recently, Mr Norton has spoken of this scene is one of his letters to the 'Times' newspaper, as a "frivolous quarrel." I leave to others to determine what the notions of general conduct towards a woman were likely to be, in the person whose ideas of "frivolous" disputes are thus exemplified. My brother's interference availed, however, for that time. Mr Norton apologised, adjured me to pardon him, and wrote triumphantly to my brother to say that we "were all right again," and that he hoped my brother also would "forget and forgive."

On occasions that really *were* "frivolous," he was not less tyrannical. His sister came to stay with us for three or four months, in London; and he notified me that I should go nowhere unless she was invited with us. I pleaded that her eccentricities prevented my friends from inviting her; that she dressed differently to other ladies; wearing a sort of Bloomer costume, a short dress with trowsers, and her hair cropped like a man's; and altogether affected masculine singularities, which astonished and repelled persons who had the usual habits of society. Mr Norton, however, held firm to his determination, and declared he would sooner "cut the traces of the carriage" than allow me to go without her.

The year after the scene of breaking open the door, my sisters, brother-in-law, and brother planned a tour in Germany, and I was very anxious to be of the party. Mr Norton consented, provided that I would defray the expense of the tour. I provided for it, by an agreement with Messrs. Saunders and Otley, for a novel called "The Wife and Woman's Reward," and we set out and joined my family at Antwerp.

We proceeded, however, no further than Aix la Chapelle, when Mr Norton became ill with a lameness which made him unwilling to travel, and the others went on without us. I defy any wife to have shown more unselfish or devoted attention to a husband, than I did to Mr Norton under these circumstances, although assured that there was not the slightest cause for anxiety in his indisposition. We were without servants—the courier and lady's maid having accompanied the main party. Mr Norton would scarcely permit any attendance from the domestics of the hotel—he spoke no foreign language, and the misunderstandings irritated him. I combined therefore in my own person, by his desire, the functions of sick-nurse, valet, and chambermaid.

I solemnly declare that there was no task, however menial or laborious, that I was not expected to perform, and did not perform. I was never allowed to go out, even for a walk. I was permitted, occasionally, to dine at the table d'hôte; and sent for, more than once, in the midst of my dinner, to be told that the meal was inconceivably long; or to be desired to put

35

leeches that had been used, into fresh water. More than one person in the hotel expressed doubts as to my being really Mr Norton's wife, in consequences of his strange treatment of me; and, at length, after some explanations with me, the German doctor volunteered to remonstrate with my husband. He told him that I was ill from over-exertion and want of fresh air; that some of the tasks imposed upon me were not only too fatiguing but positively injurious; he advised Mr Norton to employ a "garçon des bains" to wait on him instead of me, and asked permission for me to visit his wife and sister, and walk with them. I wrote to "complain," as usual, to my family, and my brother came back to me.

It will scarcely be believed that, after all this, I having, as I have stated, acted as Mr Norton's servant; having defrayed the whole expence of the dreary residence which was substituted for our tour; and being quite ill and worn out at last, with the way in which my days had passed; he took the first opportunity of again resorting to personal violence. I objected to his smoking in our little travelling carriage, especially as he smoked a hookah. I was irritated and suffocated by the volume of tobacco in so confined a space. I begged Mr Norton several times to wait till we arrived at the hotel. He did not answer of desist. At length I impatiently snatched at the pipe, and flung the mouth-piece out of the window. The carriage was then slowly ascending a hill, and Mr Norton alighted and recovered the missing portion of the pipe. He then seized me by the throat, and pinned me back with a fierce oath against the hood of the carriage. I thought then, and I think now, that I should have been strangled in a minute or two more, but that I struggled from his grasp, and without even attempting to have the carriage stopped, slipped down through the door, (which he had not closed) into the road. I ran after the other carriages, and entreated some one of my family to travel with us to protect me, which was accordingly done. The marks of his fingers were in bruises on my throat; and from the date of this foreign tour there existed an alienation from my husband on the part of my family, which his subsequent conduct completed.

Early in the ensuing summer, the quarrel, which divided

him from *them* for ever, took place. On this occasion I left Mr Norton, and withdrew to the house of my brother-in-law; and my husband desiring my return, my brother sent a friend to arrange conditions for that return, in writing; stating that till that was done he refused to enter into any correspondence whatever with Mr Norton, nor was it to be thought that any brother would permit his sister to receive the treatment I did. I was warned and earnestly advised *not* to go back, after all that had occurred; and if I had taken that advice—if I had had more resolution and less credulity—I should not now be summing up the evidence of seventeen years of torment, sorrow, and shame. But it would not have suited Mr Norton so to let me escape. He gave the written pledge of good treatment to the friend my brother had sent. He said he was willing to "make any sacrifice, provided I returned to my home." He wrote to me, entreating me not to let others divide us. He wrote to my family in the extremest and most exaggerated terms of submission. He said he was glad they had avenged me and scorned him, and he vowed to treat me kindly for the future.

To me, his letters were couched in terms of the most passionate adjuration for pity and forgiveness. They were letters it was impossible to read without being touched—they were letters which drew me home again, in spite of past deceiving, past broken promises, past ill-usage—in spite of the advice to "hold firm," and not return, which I received from almost every friend I had. I was safe; I was out of his power: my reputation was unsullied. I was with my sister; and I returned, in answer to his imploring prayers, only to be rewarded with attempted ruin and disgrace! He said "no words could prove his remorse." He said, "As there is a God above us, who will judge our actions, I think I have a right to ask you to trust me for the future. If I cannot make you happy, let us then quietly and rationally separate, I declaring to the world *that the cause of it was not any imputation on you.*" He implored me by all that was dear and holy to grant a "complete" forgiveness—a "real" pardon—to write it the moment I had read this letter—to seal and send it by post, and not to let any one see it, for fear they should advise against it.

He said, "You shall never repent of this; you shall not—you shall not." He adjured me not to "crush" him, and he ended his letter with the words, "I go on my knees to you! Have pity—have compassion on me!"

I answered him: I pitied him: I went back to him: I believed then that he really repented, and grieved to lose me; I am convinced now, that it was part of a scheme: of a determination, at least, that if we *were* to part, he would make me rue the day on my own account.

After my return, he treated me as he had done before.

As to the conditions, they were broken before I had been two days in my home: and during a very severe illness which followed the agitation and misery to which I had been exposed, and in which I prematurely lost my infant, he behaved with the utmost harshness and neglect, leaving me to be nursed by my brother, and refusing to be answerable for the expenses incurred.

Scarce a month after his last penitent and touching letter to me, my brother was again compelled to remind him that he appeared to have forgotten the reasons that made "interference on my behalf a duty," and that totally prevented his presuming to question the authority by which my brother interfered. This was in August, 1835. Things were fast driving to ruin. My family remained on the most formal and distant terms with Mr Norton, the male members of it scarcely acknowledging his acquaintance. I can call them to witness that, after our reconciliation, I pleaded for him; but it was not only on *my* account, that they close to withdraw from his intimacy.

I saw less of him than usual, during the few months that intervened before our final separation. He went alone for the shooting season to Scotland, as I was not well enough to travel, and after his return he spent nearly all the time he could command with Miss Vaughan, through whom he hoped at least to right the disorder in his pecuniary affairs. Lord Melbourne declined to make any attempt to obtain a better appointment than the one he had already bestowed; and while I was with my sister in the country, wrote to complain of a strange attempt on Mr Norton's part to interfere as to the appointment of another magistrate (in which I afterwards found he was to have a personal advantage).

I returned to town when matters were in this condition; my stay there was to have been brief, for I had settled to pass the Easter with my children at my brother's house in Dorsetshire. I was then on perfectly friendly terms with Mr Norton, in spite of his discontent in other matters. He had written me coaxing and flattering letters, urging me to try, both with Lord Melbourne and Lord John Russell, to get this appointment given to his friend, and praising "Lord M.'s kindness on all occasions." He never opposed in any way my plans for the Easter, but, on the contrary, urged me, now we were friends, to over-rule my brother's objections to receive him, and get him also invited—in which attempt I did not succeed.

On the day previous to that on which I was to leave town, I returned from my drive, and found Miss Vaughan had called in my absence, and remained closeted with my husband for some time. Lord Melbourne was with him when I came in, and they were all talking together. After Lord M. left, Mr Norton talked discontentedly of the appointment, and angrily of my not getting that and pecuniary interests arranged for him. He also said Miss Vaughan had told him, if he himself was not noticed by my brother, he ought not to submit to my going to his house with my children.

I said nothing should prevent my going to my brother; that it was Mr Norton's own fault he was not on terms with my family; that the doctor had orderd change of air for the elder child, who was recovering from scarlatina; and that I should give my servants orders to refuse Miss Vaughan admittance to my house, as she laboured always for mischief, in spite of my patience with her.

We parted angrily—Mr Norton to dine with the chief magistrate, Sir Frederic Rose, and I to dine with Lady Mary Fox. We spent the evening together at a party at Lord Harrington's, and returned home together. The dispute was then renewed, whether under the circumstances I should go to my brother's. Mr Norton's last words were—"Well, the children shall not, that I have determined;" and as he entered the house he desired the servant to unpack the carriage (which had been prepared for starting), and take the children's things out, for that they were not going. He then went up to the nursery and repeated the order to the nurse. It was admitted at the trial that the sole observation I made on this occasion, when the nurse asked me "what she was to do?" was, that *"Mr Norton's orders must be obeyed."* I neither braved him with useless words, nor complained. I waited till the morning, and then went to my sister's, to consult with her what was to be done.

While I was with my sister, my children were kidnapped and taken possession of by Miss Vaughan; as I doubt not had been agreed upon the day before. The man-servant came to my sister's, and said "something was going wrong at home;" that the children, with their things, had been put into a hackney-coach and taken away, he did not know where. I had the children traced to Miss Vaughan's house, and followed them.

Anything like the bitter insolence of this woman—who thought she had baffled and conquered me for life—I never experienced. She gave vent to the most violent and indecent answers to my reproaches, and said that if I troubled her further she would give me into the hands of the police.

I left her, and went alone to my brother's house in the country. I wished him to return immediately to town with me; and so far from having intended, previous to this outrage, to leave my home, or having made any preparation whatever for such an event, I left everything that belonged to me (even my wearing apparel) in Mr Norton's house; and he, who afterwards advertised me as a run-away, thought it so probable that I should re-appear next day with my brother, that he gave his order in writing to the man-servant, dated the morning after my departure:

> In case Mrs Norton or her brother should return to town, and call at Storey's Gate, this is my written authority to you, to refuse admittance, and to open the house-door only with the chain across.
>
> G.C. NORTON.

It was thought best that I should *not* return, and I therefore escaped the disgraceful reception with the chain across the door of my home, which my husband had prepared for me. I wrote to Mr Norton's mother, to inform her of what had occurred, and to say that I must part from him; and Mr Norton, on his side, requested Lord Harrington to write to my family to say he would part from me,—but make no provision for me,—nor suffer me to have my children.

I did not, at first, know that a mother had no legal claim to her children, and I answered by defying this injustice. My mother, my brother, and my brother-in-law, also wrote to Lord Harrington, explaining to him the truth, and disclosing to him—with very severe comments on Mr Norton's character—the circumstances of our former disputes.

Lord Harrington communicated to Mr Norton the substance of these replies (which contained proofs, extracted from Mr Norton's own letters), and told him that I utterly refused to accede to his terms. Mr Norton then said he would not part from me quietly, but endeavour publicly to disgrace me; that he had put the affair in the hands of lawyers, pledged himself not to interfere, and was not allowed to mention what they thought of doing; that my family had conspired against him, and they should maintain me; that he was occupied with enquiries into my conduct towards my male acquaintance in general, and would "try for a divorce," if a case could be made out.

In one of the attempts to "make out" a case, Mr Norton resorted to the strange *ruse* of engaging the cab-boy of the gentleman he desired to entrap, and sending the lad to try and get his master's letters from the Club; an act of which Lord Harrington observed, that *"if attempted at the Post-office, it would have been felony."*

Having reported to Lord Harrington all that could be said to my detriment, Lord H. wrote to Mr Norton as follows:—

I have told Mrs N. all the base calumnies uttered against her. I will do the same by you. They say that you kept a mistress. They say that you wanted to borrow *1,440l.* from Lord Melbourne; that you accepted favors from Lord—, after professing jealousy of him. That you pledged your word of honour to a falsehood. That your wife made by her writing a sum more than sufficient to pay all your debts. That you have yourself denied her to visitors, and even to members of her own family, when Lord Melbourne has been with her. Unless you can disprove these accusations, you are lost in the estimation of the world.

Lord Harrington then wrote to me, as follows:—

I called next day. I was received by a Mr Maclean; a lawyer and friend. Mr Maclean said, it was agreed that Norton should see no one. I talked over these 'accusations' with Mr M. I challenged him to answer them. He said, 'This is not the time, and you are not the person.' I said, 'You cannot answer them.' I wrote afterwards to Norton as follows:—'I now see clearly that you are surrounded by a clique of lawyers and friends, and under their influence, who keep your person and your mind imprisoned. Put your jailors to the test. Let them answer the accusations in my letter, and let them answer this additional charge. You are accused (not by me) of having intended to procure a Magistracy for a gentleman for a compensation in money. Ask your lawyers and the friends who influence them, if this charge were proved, whether you would be allowed to sit on the judgment seat.

L.S.

To these adjurations Lord Harrington received no more satisfactory reply from Mr Norton, than the following careless allusion in a letter on the general subject of our quarrel.

As regards the 'on dits,' stated in yours, this does not appear to be the time to enter upon that refutation of them which I should otherwise court an opportunity of obtaining.
Ever yours,
G.C. Norton.
April, 14th, 1836.

Mr Norton did not, however, seem to build with certainty on the chance of refutation; for his next step was to request an interview with Sir James Graham (who was related to me by my mother's side), and inform him that he admitted his lawyers could prove nothing amiss in my conduct, and that, therefore, he was willing to come to such terms of separation as could be agreed upon. Sir James Graham demanded, as a preliminary to all negociation, *a written retraction of the slanders against me.* What was Mr Norton's reply? That he believed them? No: but that "if he retracted what was said of me, would my family contradict what was said of him, as otherwise he would be left in his wife's power?"

Sir James Graham would not discuss this condition, but left Mr Norton to his reflections, promising to see him again. The painful scandal was supposed to be ended, and Lord Harrington wrote thus to congratulate me:

22nd April, 1836.

Thank God your persecutors have terminated their labours. Their object was not truth or justice; not to examine into your character, but solely to criminate you. It has ended in your honour and their disgrace. N's conduct is really disreputable; but far less so than those who have hunted him on.

Most premature were these congratulations! At the very time when Mr Norton was angrily wavering between the dread of exposure for himself, and the desire of vengeance, certain personages, who saw in our quarrel an opportunity for a stroke in politics, persuaded him to attack Lord Melbourne.

I know Mr Norton has denied that he was thus advised; especially by his friend and guardian Lord Wynford. I know that he made the incredible assertion, that his sole-adviser was a stable-helper, whom he himself had formerly discharged for drunkenness, and who was, at the time of this quarrel, a rag-seller in Monmouth-street; that this man suddenly appeared, and told him a gross and strange story, on the strength of which he made up his mind to prosecute the Prime Minister of England.

Let those believe this history who can; it is certainly *possible* that all that was said of the interference of political leaders, was as false as what they said of me; but, meanwhile, I know that the late King considered it a political plot; that Lord Melbourne himself thought so; that some of the witnesses affirmed they had been examined in Lord Wynford's house; and that, at all events, the impression of some such interference obtained sufficiently to make the Duke of Cumberland anxious to deny it on behalf of the Tory party, as Lord Melbourne's letters will prove.

In the preceding year the Whigs had been turned out; Sir Robert Peel had been sent for in all haste from Italy, to form a Tory administration; and the new Government had been immediately outvoted on Lord John Russell's Church Temporalities Bill. In May, Lord Melbourne reconstructed a Whig Cabinet, and the Ministry of a moment found themselves again in the ranks of the opposition; an opposition notoriously in possession of the sympathy of the Court. In the letters lately published by Mr Norton, he has himself branded the conduct of the case got up against the unwelcome Whig Minister, by revealing the minutes of his own lawyer's consultation with Sir William Follett. By these minutes it is shown, that Sir W.F. considered the character of the witnesses so bad, that he doubted the probability of a verdict being obtained; but that, nevertheless, they thought it worth while to proceed at all hazards, *for the sake of the exposure.* It is made perfectly clear that some of those concerned in this business, were careless what might be the result, so long as there was an overwhelming public scandal; and as to Mr Norton himself, his conduct was infinitely less rash and unreasonable than the event would make it appear; since he has over and over again admitted, that he had a secret reliance the case *would not be defended at all.*

He,—who alone knew how miserable my home had been, —how often I had threatened to leave him,—how but a very few months before, I had put that threat into execution by withdrawing to my sister's house, and had only been lured home again, by his exaggerated protestations of repentance and despair,—*he* believed, that I would not unwillingly renounce that bitter union, and existence of perpetual struggle, to become the wife of Lord Melbourne. He thought he saw a golden path out of all his difficulties; freedom from the marriage tie; pecuniary damages from the Prime Minister; and the power of avenging, by my disgrace, the scorn formerly shewn him by my family. Those who had instigated him, came to the trial doubtful of the result, but confident of the scandal; Mr Norton came to it, careless of the scandal, and confident of the result. He miscalculated his chances, only because the trial was defended.

The mockery of accusation was gone through; Mr Norton was represented as an amiable, injured, deceived husband; Lord Melbourne as a profligate impostor; and I myself as a painted wanton. The time which had been spent in reading translations of Aeschylus—listening to explanations of the unknown theories of politics,—

> And search of deep philosophy,
> Wit, eloquence, and poesy.

was represented to have been passed in a manner which amazed me less by the falsehood than the coarseness of the invention. The groom-ragseller came into court dead-drunk:* other witnesses were proved to be lost characters: cross-examination elicited that they had received money, and had actually resided till the time of trial at the country seat of Lord Grantley. The whole evidence stopped short three years before the actual period of trial, as they dared not call any *but* these witnesses.

The jury listened with open incredulity and disgust to the evidence, and without requiring to hear a single witness for Lord Melbourne, or leaving the jury-box, they instantly gave their verdict against Mr Norton: a verdict which was received with cheers which the Judge vainly attempted to suppress. The impression generally made on the public mind, I give from the letter of Mr David Leahy to Mr Power, who sent it to my younger brother:

> As I was present during the whole exhibition, I can take it upon me as an impartial spectator to say, that a more infamous case on the part of the plaintiff, never came before a court of justice. All the world—whatever their politics may be, or whatever their opinions about the discretion of the behaviour of all or either of the three principal parties,—must acknow-

---

*See Appendix.

ledge that the principal witnesses were perjured and suborned. I have spoken with almost every person present, and
there exists a perfect unanimity upon this point. The jury,
upon the close of the plaintiff's case, intimated, in a manner
perfectly intelligible to the initiated, that it was a mere super-
fluity to set up any defence. They shewed the greatest impatience during the Attorney-General's speech, and made several attempts to interrupt the Judge's charge; and at last, when
it came to their own turn to take the business in hand, they
exclaimed unanimously, without a quarter of a minute's consultation or deliberation, that they found for the defendant.

The case presented altogether a combination of ridiculous
driftless futility, with atrocious and incredible perjury, which
cannot, I think, be paralleled (in their combination) in the
annals of criminal jurisprudence.

The printed law reports of the day give the result thus:

The Learned Judge summed up at considerable length, and the Jury
having turned round, *in a moment* the Foreman said—"My Lord, we are all
agreed—we find for the *Defendant.*"

There was a loud and general burst of applause at the announcement of
the verdict, which was instantly checked by the court.

The news was communicated outside, and was followed by loud and
general cheering from the anxious crowds assembled.

And in another paper:

The Learned Judge summed up at some length.

The Jury having turned round, *and conferred a few seconds,*—the Foreman said,—"My Lord, we are agreed,—it is my duty to say that our verdict is
for the Defendant."

The announcement was received with loud bursts of applause; an expression of feeling which was prompty re-echoed by shouts from the mob
without the doors. The tumult having been partially suppressed, the Lord
Chief Justice said "he was surprised to hear a verdict received in a court of
justice in so disgraceful a manner."

The court was then cleared.

That impression availed—for Lord Melbourne. For him,
the ordeal was happily and triumphantly over; the sympathy
of friends, the enthusiasm of the public, greeted his acquittal
from the false charge which was to wreck him. He continued

Minister to the King, and the dawn of another reign saw him confirmed in his position, with the added distinction of seeming almost the guide and guardian of the youthful Sovereign who was to receive from him her first initiation into the cares and tasks of government.

My humbler destiny was not so easily set right. Previous to the trial, I had been strenuously urged, by some of the truest friends I had, to be beforehand with Mr Norton; and, knowing what my home had been, to attempt to divorce *him* while he was preparing to accuse me. Others, equally anxious for my welfare, earnestly counselled the exact contrary: to wait,—to have patience,—to depend on the truth being shown on the trial, and my justification being then made complete. The case being submitted to Dr Lushington, he advised that I should remain passive, and I did so; sore against my will.

After the trial was over, I consulted whether a divorce "by reason of cruelty" might not be pleaded for me; and I laid before my lawyers the many instances of violence, injustice, and ill-usage, of which the trial was but the crowning example. I was then told that no divorce I could obtain would break my marriage; that I could not plead cruelty *which I had forgiven*; that by returning to Mr Norton I had "*condoned*" all I complained of. I learnt, too, the *Law* as to my children— that the right was with the father; that neither my innocence or his guilt could alter it; that not even his giving them into the hands of a mistress, would give me any claim to their custody. The eldest was but six years old, the second four, the youngest two and a half, when we were parted. I wrote, therefore, and *petitioned* the father and husband, in whose power I was, for leave to see them—for leave to keep them, till they were a little older. Mr Norton's answer was, that I should not have them; that if I wanted to see them, I might have an interview with them at the chambers of his attorney. I refused, and wrote as follows to my solicitor, who had conveyed his decision to me:

> However bitter it may be to me, I must decline seeing my children in the manner proposed. I say nothing of the harshness, the inhumanity of telling me I must either see them at the

chambers of his solicitor, or not at all; but I say it is not *decent* that the father of those children should force me, their mother, out of the very tenderness I bear them, to visit them at the chambers of the attorney who collected the evidence, examined the witnesses, and conducted the proceedings for the intended divorce. I say it is not decent—nay, that even if I were guilty, it would not be decent to make me such a proposal. But I am innocent. I have been pronounced innocent by a jury of my countrymen—I have been solemnly and publicly declared innocent by the nobleman against whom that ill-advised action was brought, Why, then, are my children kept from me?—from me whom even their own witnesses proved to be a careful and devoted mother? Mr Norton says, the Law gives him my children. I know it does, but the Law does no more; it does not compel me to endure more than separation from them; and sooner than allow them to connect my visits in their memory with secresy and shame, I would submit never again to behold them till they were of an age to visit me without asking permission of any human being.

More than once, Mr Norton's advisers have shown more feeling for me than my husband himself; and on this occasion his solicitor wrote:—"Mr Norton has made the appointment to see the children here—I cannot but regret it."

Eventually, the children were permitted to come to my brother's house; Mr Norton expressly limiting the time of their stay to one half-hour, and sending them with two of the women who had been witnesses on the trial, who stated that their "orders" were to remain in the room with me. I was not allowed even to see my baby of two years old without these "*witnesses.*"

What I suffered on my children's account, none will ever know or measure. "The heart knoweth its own bitterness," and God knew mine! The days and nights of tears and anguish, that grew into the struggle of years—it is even *now* a pain to me to look back upon: even *now*, the hot agony of resentment and grief rises in my mind, when I think of the needless tyranny I endured in this respect. Mr Norton held my children as hostages; he felt that while he had them, he still had a power over me that nothing could control. Baffled in the matter of the trial and damages, he had still the power to do more than punish—to torture—the wife who had been so anxious to part from him. I never saw them; I seldom knew where they were.

Once, when I wrote to ask after them in illness, my letter to the nurse (which contained no syllable of offence, or beyond the subject of my inquiry) was turned inside out, and franked back to me. Miss Vaughan was dead, and I appealed to my mother-in-law (with whom I heard my husband meant to place them), entreating her to refuse to take them; which she promised to do, and heard me with tears of sympathy. But my husband's sister, Lady Menzies decided differently: to her, on payment of so much a head, my three children were consigned; and removed to Scotland, where neither their father nor I could be with them. There, with one whom I knew to be haughty and intemperate, those children were left, who had hitherto been so gently and tenderly treated; and the eldest of whom was delicate in health, sensitive in disposition, and just recovering from illness.

The first step she made in their education, was to flog this very child (a child of six years old) for merely receiving and reading a letter from me (I being in England and he in Scotland), to "impress on his memory" that he was not to receive letters from me. Having occasion to correct one still younger, she stripped it naked, tied it to the bed-post, and chastised it with a riding-whip. She was a fit sister and colleague to Mr Norton; and I have lived to see the day when *her* disputes for money, with her own sons, have come to Scotch law-pleadings; as Mr Norton has brought to English law-pleadings the like disputes with us.

These boys having been the gleam of happiness and compensation in my home, it was not to be supposed I would give them up without a struggle, because it was so "written in the bond" of the English law. Ceaselessly, restlessly, perseveringly, I strove; and, fortunately for me, other cases of hardship had already drawn attention to the necessity of some reform on this subject; especially the case of a Mrs Greenhill, in which Serjeant Talfourd (now Sir Thomas Noon Talfourd) had been professionally concerned. A new "Infant Custody Bill" was brought forward by the learned Serjeant; and

49

passed, after a struggle of three years, by a majority of four to one. As soon as it had passed, I prepared affidavits to lay before the Chancellor; and again Mr Norton narrowly escaped exposure.

Among the persons on whom I depended as a witness of past events was the Right Hon. Edward Ellice. When he was applied to for an affidavit, he thought it a merciful wisdom to warn Mr Norton of what he could prove, and to endeavour to prevent the raking-up of affairs which had begun to be forgotten by the public. Mr Norton answered boldly:—

> Police Court, Whitechapel, Nov. 27, 1841
> ...I have long looked to the threatened proceedings as the only mode of attaining a settlement, and of unmasking the repeated unwarrantable and hitherto unresisted attacks which have been perseveringly made on my character for some years.

But when he had had an interview with Mr Ellice; and had learned *what* that friend was expected to prove, he hastily retracted; and signified to me through his lawyers that it was unnecessary for me to present a petition on affidavit, as he yielded the point, and would not defend himself.

He yielded—simply so far as the law would have compelled him, and as was necessary to save himself from the threatened and certain exposure which my appeal under the new law would have entailed. I saw my children in the most formal and comfortless manner. There was no mercy or generosity. I expected none. He even made it a personal quarrel with his colleague and fellow magistrate, Mr Hardwicke, after this, that Mr H. had permitted me one evening to be in his box at the play, with my children. He locked the children themselves up for a whole day; to punish them; and "impress upon their memories" (after the fashion of his sister), that they were not to be seen with me at any public place. Their interviews with me, were to be *in private*; that no one might know or guess he had been compelled to yield. The insane injustice of punishing the children, or quarrelling with the friend who had catered for their amusement, when no one intended to offend him, never seems to have occurred to him. He feared only the truth being known; our appearance in public, was a contradiction of his assertions in private.

His cruel carelessness was afterwards proved, on a most miserable occasion. My youngest child, then a boy of eight years old, left without care or overlooking, rode out with a brother but little older than himself, was thrown, carried to the house of a country neighbour, and died there of lock-jaw, consequent on the accident. Mr Norton allowed the child to lie ill for a week—indeed to be at death's door—before he sent to inform me. Sir Fitzroy and Lady Kelly were staying with Mr Norton in the country. Lady Kelly (who was an utter stranger to me) met me at the railway station. I said—"I am here,—is my boy better?" "No," she said—"he is not better—he is dead." And I found, instead of my child, a corpse already coffined.

Mr Norton asked my forgiveness then, as he had asked it often before; he sent his elder child to plead for him,—for well he knew what my children were to me; he humbled himself, and grieved for an hour, till he changed into pity the horror and repugnance I had expressed at the idea of seeing him;—and then he buried our child, and forgot both his sorrow and his penitence.

———————

III

During the years over which my separation from these children extended, several attempts were made by Mr Norton either to compel me to his own terms, or to bring about a reconciliation. In the Spring immediately following the Trial (after my first efforts to obtain my children had been rejected) I suddenly received from him a most extraordinary note, saying, that he considered our difference "*capable of adjustment,*" and hoped I would meet him alone, in an empty house, No. 1 Berkeley street, where he would wait for me. I received this communication with doubt and distrust; increased rather than diminished by the impatience shown by Mr Norton to obtain an answer, for which he sent twice in the course of the afternoon. He then wrote to say, that "nothing could be effected without mutual confidence," and as he could not come to my uncle's house (where I lived) he hoped I would come to his own residence. This I consented to do. We had a long wretched interview. He besought me once more, to "forget the past" and return home. He laid the blame of all that had happened, on his friends and advisers; said the trial was against his will and judgment, and that he longed to "take me to his heart again." He complained of the coldness with which I received these proposals; but I did not refuse. He recalled my poor children from Scotland; and sent notes almost daily to my house. Those letters began, "My Carry," "My dear Carry," and were signed, "Yours affectionately." Two of them (in allusion to my fear of meeting him) bore the playful signature of "*Greenacre,*"—the name of a man who had been recently hung, for enticing a woman to his house by promising marriage, and then murdering and cutting her into pieces.

After a month of this strange correspondence, I received a note from him, to say that his sister had arrived to stay with him. A dispute followed, as to what I had or had not said to this lady. Mr Norton complained that I had stated to her I did not intend "honestly" to return to him; but "to return *for the sake of my children and my reputation*;" and that I had said, "I never would live with him again." Our reconciliation was broken off; my children were sent back to Scotland; and the next notice taken of my existence, by the husband who had wooed my return,—who had begged me to meet him in an empty house, assuring me nothing could be effected "without mutual confidence;"—who had signed himself *Greenacre*, in familiar and caressing letters, jesting upon my fears and doubts as to trusting myself alone at the meeting;—and who had, in the first instance, desired his servant the day after my departure, to open the door of my home "with the chain across;"—the next step, I say, taken by the husband whose real story was so little known to the public, was to impose on that public by an advertisement respecting his legal liability for me, commencing,—

Whereas on 30th March, 1836, my wife, Caroline Elizabeth Sarah, left me, her family, and home, and hath from thenceforth continued to live separate and apart from me, &c.

Angry, and full of scorn, I consulted my solicitor whether I was compelled to bear this fresh outrage. I showed him the letters Mr N. had written, just before this pretence of being a forsaken husband:—"Have I no remedy?"—"No remedy in *Law*. The *Law* can do nothing for you: your case is one of singular, of incredible hardship; but there is no possible way in which the *Law* could assist you." My brother did all that could be done—he desired his solicitors to publish a letter stating that "the whole of the statements contained in Mr Norton's advertisement were false"—an imputation which remains on it to this day.

After the insult of the advertisement, there was a pause of some weeks; and then Mr Norton wrote to say he wished an arbitration in our affairs; the arbitrator he named was Sir

John Bayley; and as the history of the reference is given later, I do not here enter into it; futher than to say, that Mr Norton, after solemnly pledging himself in writing, to abide by whatever decision might be come to, utterly refused to be bound; quarrelled with his arbitrator; and broke off the negotiation. A year and a half afterwards, he requested Sir Frederick Thesiger to act as referee; whose opinion I give in his own words:

> The accommodation proposed by Norton is one in which you are to give way upon every subject, and he is not to recede upon one; and it seems to me to be ridiculous to talk of conciliation upon such a footing... It is impossible not to be struck with the vacillating and vexatious course which Norton has pursued; exciting hopes only to disappoint them, and making promises apparently for the opportunity of breaking them.

Friends mediated; men of business wasted their time in vain; Mr Norton's promises were ropes of sand.

In 1842—two years after Mr Norton had evaded the chance of exposure by declining to defend my petition under the Infant Custody Bill—he once more asked me to be "reconciled" to him, and to return and live with him. Though this was not arranged, yet from that time there was a degree of peace and friendliness established, which, for the sake of my sons (of whom I had already lost one), I was more than willing—I was anxious—to maintain.

Mr Norton's letters again became caressing and flattering; he visited me at the house of my uncle Mr C. Sheridan, and after Mr Sheridan's death, at my own. When I wrote to him from abroad, in 1848, he sent one of my letters triumphantly to my mother, to prove to her what good terms we were on. He followed me to Germany, and said he did not think I ought to "travel alone." Down to the time of my mother's death, and the dispute respecting her annuity,—whatever under-current of bitterness and distrust there might be on my part, or of caprice on his—we remained on familiar and friendly terms; and he relapsed into the old habit of entreating my interference for his interests, with such of my family or friends as had political influence; as he had done when we lived together in one home.

The history of the contract—in the dispute about which, after my mother's death, this state of things was broken up—I have given separately; but before I conclude those pages which treat of the past instead of the present, I think it is fit to show, by the evidence of Lord Melbourne's own letters, the opinion *he* entertained of those affairs, in which his name has been once more introduced by Mr Norton as an opportunity for falsehood.

IV

The first letter I shall quote of Lord Melbourne's, is one written only *three months* after he had given Mr Norton his magistracy; when already he was disturbed at the conduct of his nominee. Mr Norton inaugurated his appointment by quarrelling with his colleague. I endeavoured to justify my husband; and blamed the other magistrate. Lord Melbourne replied thus; in a letter dated July 19, 1831; and I print it, because it is a curious prophetic comment on Mr Norton's late letters in the 'Times.'

Home Office, July 19th, 1831.
T.W., as you say, does what he has not the least right to do; and the worst is, he is not only foolish himself, but is the cause of folly in others. I had the greatest difficulty in preventing Norton from replying to him in the 'Times.' I was much alarmed at the notion of his doing this, especially as I found him thoroughly impressed with the opinion that he could do it with great cleverness and dexterity. Now I know very well that a man of that description who is fully persuaded that he is about to do a thing extremely well, is on the very point of committing some irretrievable error, or falling into some most ridiculous absurdity . . I hate the magistrates writing to the newspapers . . besides, people will be sure to say to me,—if the magistrates get squabbling in public, why do you not clear the bench of these fellows altogether? A question to which I should not well know what to reply. They tell me also, that Norton does not go to his office early enough. I should be annoyed at having a complaint made upon this subject. Pray dissuade him, gently, from any public exhibitions in the newspapers; and urge him gently to a little more activity in the morning. He might surely without difficulty get there by twelve o'clock. This is a disagreeable lecturing letter, but still upon matters to which it is necessary to pay some attention.

Good natured and familiar as was this expression of dissatisfaction, I felt that Lord Melbourne was beginning to perceive the character of the husband for whom I had successfully petitioned; and I warned—and warned in vain. To the last, however, Mr Norton relied on Lord Melbourne's kindness; and the next note I shall give, is a curious and explicit answer to the assertions of my husband, as to his jealousy and unhappiness; for it is dated only eight weeks before *our final separation*, and discusses the appointment Mr Norton had agreed to endeavour to obtain; (his pertinacity about which appears to have puzzled the Home Office.)

Downing street, January 27th, 1836.
Norton plagues me to death about the successor to Walker. He seems to think that he and H. have almost a right to make the appointment. He has just brought me a letter, strongly recommending a Mr—, and seemed to be struck as with a new idea, when I told him that he had better let me mention the name to Lord John as from myself; inasmuch as he and H. interfering, would rather be against the candidate, than for him. He seems to think that everything is to give way to the consideration of giving him a pleasant compassion. He says the Bench used with Walker to be like a pleasant club, and that he must have an agreeable fellow to walk to and fro with. Now do not try to stop him, nor give him any notion of what I have said. I wrote to you yesterday about F. I am told by those who know him that he certainly would not accept it. Adieu,
Yours, Melbourne.

Two months afterwards, Mr Norton and I were parted: Lord Melbourne passed the Easter at Broeke and Panshanger; and as *I* never dreamed that he would himself be made the pretence of our quarrel, I wrote to tell him what had happened. I quote four of his letters written at that time. Living, he justified himself by his simple word of honour; and dead, I justify him with lines written by a hand cold in the grave. However deservedly severe his language may be with respect to Mr Norton, I leave those who read, to judge whether these are the letters of a treacherous seducer,—or even of a lover.

Panshanger, April 6th, 1836.

...I hardly know what to write to you, or what comfort to offer. You know, as well as I do, that the best course is to keep yourself tranquil, and not to give way to feelings and passions which Heaven knows are too natural to be easily resisted. This conduct upon his part seems perfectly unaccountable; and depend upon it, being, as you are, in the right, it will be made ultimately to appear, whatever temporary misrepresentations may prevail. You cannot have better or more affectionate advisers than you have with you upon the spot, who are well acquainted with the circumstances of the case, and with the characters of those with whom they have to deal. You know that I have always counselled you to bear everything, and remain to the last. I thought it for the best. I am afraid it is no longer possible. Open breaches of this kind are always to be lamented; but you have the consolation that you have done your utmost to stave this extremity off as long as possible. In all difficulties you may always depend upon me, and believe in me,

Yours, Melbourne.

Panshanger, April 8, 1836.

...It is in vain to rail, otherwise I could do so too; but it was at all times easy to see that it was the most dangerous and ill-conditioned creature possible, and that there was nothing that might not be expected from such a mixture of folly and malignity. I am very glad C. is gone down. You have now real friends about you. You describe me very truly when you say that I am always more annoyed that there is a row than sorry for the persons engaged in it. But, after all, you know you can count upon me. I wonder that you should think it possible that I should communicate your letters to any one else; I have heard no one mention the subject. Lord Holland did, in one of his letters, and I answered him exactly to the effect you told me, and as I must have done without being told, namely, that I had seen you with Norton the day before you left town, and that I knew that he was perfectly well acquainted with your intention of going into the country,* because he, in my hearing, suggested putting it off from Wednesday, I believe, until

---

* There was a report that I had eloped, sedulously circulated by Mr Norton's friends.

59

Saturday. I have also seen one paragraph relating to the matter in one of the newspapers, and this is all that has reached me. I shall be in town again on Monday. Adieu.

Yours, Melbourne.

Panshanger, April 10th, 1836.

I have just received your letter, with Leicester Stanhope's enclosed, with which I am much pleased. He could not have acted better, nor with more discretion. Never, to be sure, was there such conduct! To set on foot that sort of enquiry without the slightest real ground for it! But it does not surprise me. I have always known that there was there a mixture of folly and violence which might lead to any absurdity or any injustice. You know so well my opinion, that it is unnecessary for me to repeat it. I have always told you that a woman should never part from her husband whilst she can remain with him. If this is generally the case, it is particularly so in such a case as yours: that is, in the case of a young handsome woman, of lively imagination, fond of company and conversation, and whose celebrity and superiority have necessarily created many enemies. Depend upon it, if a reconciliation is feasible, there can be no doubt of the prudence of it. It is so evident that it is unnecessary to expatiate upon it. Lord Holland, who is almost the only person who has mentioned the subject to me, is entirely of that opinion.

Yours, Melbourne.

South street, April 1836.

...If, for the sake of your children, you think you can endure to return to him, you certainly will act most wisely and prudently for yourself in doing so. I advise you, however, to take no step of yourself without the advice of Seymour and Graham; and if you determine upon writing to Mr Barlow, send your letter open to them, giving them a discretionary power either to send or to withhold it.

Keep up your spirits; agitate yourself as little as possible; do not be too anxious about rumours and the opinion of 'the World;' being (as you are) innocent and in the right, you will, in the end, bring everything round.

Yours, Melbourne.

These four letters were all written before it occurred to Mr

60

Norton, or had been suggested to him, to speculate on the advantage of making Lord Melbourne *himself* appear the cause of our quarrel, by bringing an action against him. The chances were all favourable; for either large damages would be given, if successful, or, if the scandal was one of the Prime Minister dared not face, probably a large sum might be given as a compromise to prevent the suit being brought at all. The astounding intelligence having been communicated to Lord Melbourne; I received from him the following note.

South street, April 23rd, 1836.

I send you a letter which I wrote yesterday with the intention of sending it. I hope you will not take it ill, if I implore you to try, at least, to be calm under these trials. You know that what is alleged (if it be alleged) is utterly false. *And what is false can rarely be made to appear true.* The steps which it will be prudent to take, it will be impossible to determine until we know more certainly the course that is intended to be pursued. If any servant of mine, or any one that has left within the last six years had been interrogated, I think I should have heard of it. But, whoever may be interrogated, no one can depose anything which can affect you or me.

Yours, Melbourne.

South street, June 9, 1836.

I have received your letter, and have given such instructions as I trust will be for the best. I do not wonder at the impression made upon you.* I knew it would be so; and therefore I was almost unwilling to have the interview take place. All the attorneys that I have ever seen, have all the same manner; hard, cold, incredulous, distrustful, sarcastic, and sneering. They are accustomed to be conversant with the worst part of human nature, and with the most discreditable transactions. They have so many falsehoods told them, that they place confidence in none.

---

* I had written to complain of the manner of Mr Vizard, Lord Melbourne's solicitor, who came to question me, and did not appear to belive me, when I asserted my innocence. I said the accusation was nothing against Lord M. (according to the views taken in society of the conduct of men;) but that it was life and death to me, as a woman; and that I would not see Mr Vizard at all, if he insulted me by expressions of incredulity.

I have sent your note, having read it. I dare say you think me unfeeling; but I declare that since I first heard I was able to be proceeded against, I have suffered more intensely than I ever did in my life. I had neither sleep nor appetite, and I attribute the whole of my illness (at least of the severity of it) to the uneasiness of my mind. Now what is this uneasiness for? Not for my own character, because, as you justly say, the imputation upon me is as nothing. It is not for the political consequences to myself, although I deeply feel the consequences which my indiscretion may bring upon those who are attached to me and follow my fortunes. The real and principal object of my anxiety and solicitude is you, and the situation in which you have been so unjustly placed, by the circumstances which have taken place.

Lord Melbourne was right, so far that what was "false" was *not* made to "appear true: and that the drunken and worthless witnesses were discredited by the Jury. The very fact, however, of the utter disbelief with which the evidence was received, saved Mr Norton from any further exposure than that of having brought forward a story it was obvious even he himself could not have believed. For—as it was not thought necessary to call any witnesses to rebut the coarse invention of the accuser—our real history remained unknown as before.

The next steps taken, prove only how heartily ashamed every one was of being supposed to have had any share in the transaction. The papers of the day were filled with severe comments and counter comments. Lord Wynford denied having had any hand in the business. Lord Grantley (who at least had the excuse for the interference that he was Mr Norton's brother) partly denied it. Sir W. Follett hastened to intrench himself within the narrowest limit of professional and compulsory assistance, and published a denial of having *advised* the trial, in the 'Times;' and Lord Melbourne had already written to me, as follows, of the denial of the Duke of Cumberland.

South street.
.... What I wanted to tell you was this: that a few days ago

62

the Duke of Cumberland came up to me in one of the lobbies of the House of Lords, and said "Have you seen Wynford? He wishes to speak to you; and it is in order to assure you, upon his honour, that he has had nothing to do with this affair. Nor indeed *any of us*. We would do nothing so ungentlemanlike. The moment I heard he was charged with it, I went to him, and asked him, and he solemnly denied it." I replied that 'I never believed mere rumours and reports; that I had never thought it, and that His Royal Highness's declaration was of course, perfectly satisfactory.' When I went into the House of Lords, Lord Wynford sent one of the Messengers to ask me to come over to him, as, being lame, he could not come to me. I went, and he then repeated the disclaimer already made by the Duke of Cumberland; and added, that he 'had never heard of the action until four days after it had been commenced, and that as to that unfortunate young man'—(as he termed Norton), who he said had been his ward,—he had not seen him for these two or three years (I will not be certain of the precise time he mentioned, but it was a long one). I, of course, declared myself 'perfectly satisfied.'

Of course. A gentleman, called upon to accept the disclaimer of other gentlemen, one of them a Prince of the blood Royal, could do no less; and of all men, the two in question might feel sympathy for persons struggling against accusation; for the Duke of Cumberland had himself been the theme of resisted obloquy, in that strange history of the murder of his servant; and Lord Wynford's justice, as Judge Best, had been impugned by Lord Denman in the House of Lords, for brow-beating and unfairly fining a prisoner; not to mention other scandals, less publicly arraigned.

Lord Melbourne then, had to profess himself "satisfied," as a matter of course; but *I* was not satisfied. In the first place I knew it was not true that Lord Wynford had not seen Mr Norton for three years; and I was assured that some of the witnesses had been examined at his house. As to the denial of the Duke of Cumberland—both Princes and Kings may be eagerly served, without accepting the responsibility of their words; and the trivial task of breaking up a Ministry, need not weigh on the conscience like the riddance of St Thomas à Beckett. His Royal Highness's dissatisfaction at the success of the Whig party, and his dislike of its leader, were patent and unconcealed. Even those who were friends and adherents of that party, were involved in the evidence of that dislike. I well remember, when I attended the Court receptions, even before the event of the Mock-Trial, when it was merely surmised that I had influence with the Whig Premier, that the Duke of Cumberland was the only Royal personage who refused to acknowledge, by the slightest salute, the curtsey I made to him, as to others in the Royal circle. I mentioned it to Lord Melbourne. He said, "You take these slights to yourself, but they are not put upon *you*."

It so happened, by some strange hazard, that in the list of the jury on the trial, the name of Sir Robert Peel was called;* and Sir W. Follett took the opportunity of alluding to that circumstance in his address: he said—

> He cared not for the political sentiments of those he addressed—he would as soon have twelve political opponents as twelve supporters of his noble client, as he was sure they would do justice to both parties. There was left on the Jury the leader of the political party opposed to his client, but he would as soon have seen Sir Robert Peel in that box, as any other gentleman; and neither Lord Melbourne nor those who advised him, ever thought of objecting to that gentleman.

Certainly not; but between impeaching a leader whose honour never was attacked, and utterly acquitting *all* members of the Tory party, there is a wide gulf; and after the denials, more or less angry, and more or less positive, made publicly by persons at the time, the newspapers still debated the subject; and still boldly put the question,—"*Who then is the man behind the screen?*" The very wording of the Duke of Cumberland's denial,—the very expression, "*nor indeed* ANY OF US,"—assumed that Lord Melbourne suspected *some* of the Tory party were the real movers in the extraordinary, unexpected, and unfair attack made upon him. I repeat that I

---

* Lords Grantley, Lichfield, and Lucan were seated on the bench. Sir R. Peel and Mr F. Baring, M.P., whose names were on the Jury list, were called, but did not answer.—*Law Report*, 1836.

know the late King thought so; and as for Lord Melbourne and myself, how could it seem otherwise than a plot? He knew, and I knew (however deceived the public might be), that he was *not* the cause of the domestic rupture which had taken place. He knew, and I knew, that to the very last day and hour of my stay under my husband's roof, he had been, not only a welcome, but a peculiarly courted guest of Mr Norton's; that, to the last, favours had been begged of him, and friendliness sustained; that for years his portrait had lain, unchallenged, the principal ornament of our drawing-room table, and that I had never imagined it necessary to conceal from my husband, or any one else, the profound enthusiasm and regard I felt for that gifted and intellectual friend,—who was of my father's generation, not mine.

Lord Melbourne himself laid much stress on the admission of the witnesses, that they had received a weekly stipend, from an agent. He always considered they had been suborned, and in one of his notes alludes thus to the man Fluke:*—

July 3, 1836.

We are told that the witness 'Fluke,' made the most of the advantages of his situation whilst it lasted, and tyrannized over his employers unmercifully. He would not leave Guildford until he had had both chicken and duckling for his breakfast, and insisted upon coming up in a chaise and four. It is a pity that we did not know these circumstances upon the day of trial.

Yours, Melbourne.

Who the "employers" were,—was the only doubt; and it was that doubt which the Duke of Cumberland endeavoured to clear away—when he denied, on behalf of the whole Tory party, any undue or ungentlemanlike interference in the affair. Nevertheless, when, after the Mock-Trial, I re-appeared at the English Court (which was not without

---

* I have thought it worth while to re-print, in an Appendix, at the end of this pamphlet, part of the sworn evidence of this man; let those who read it judge for themselves of the case so supported.

express sanction, and subsequent to Her Majesty's marriage), my re-appearance was made a party question; and one or two of the Tory ladies, known to be on especial terms of familiar friendship with the Duke of Cumberland (then King of Hanover), openly boasted, that in their own little set of Royal and Political personages, they would treat the jury verdict of twelve untitled English gentlemen, as *"non avenu;"* that the Whig ladies, and such personal friends as I might have on the Tory side, might do what they pleased; but that even if the Court itself supported the verdict of acquittal, it would require only a little time and patience (on the principle laid down by Sir R. Peel, that those who could personally approach the Queen must necessarily influence Her Majesty), to bring about a change. I know this boast was especially made by a lady, whose husband has since held Court appointments, and who sedulously cultivated many Royal friendships. And that such assumption was not considered— among her own party, at least—"the baseless fabric of a vision," is certainly proved by the stress laid, in May 1839, on the privilege of dismissing all the Queen's ladies, except such as were under the rank of Ladies of the Bedchamber. The Royal decision was afterwards made public.—

Buckingham Palace, May 10th, 1839.

The Queen having considered the proposal made to her yesterday by Sir Robert Peel to remove the ladies of her Bedchamber, cannot consent to adopt a course which she conceives to be contrary to usage, and which is repugnant to her feelings.—

Sir Robert's reply was a respectfully worded refusal to take office with that restriction. In the Ministerial explanation of May 13th, 1839, he expressly stated, that—

no question arose as to the formation of the administration, or as to the principles on which the Government was to be formed or conducted. The difficulty related exclusively to that portion of the household which is filled by the LADIES in Her Majesty's service. Her Majesty conceded what could be wished or expected with respect to that part of the household which is filled by noblemen or gentlemen holding seats in either House of Parliament. The difficulty arose with respect to certain portions of that part of the establishment which is filled by the *ladies* of the household.

The influence which the Tory ladies expected to exercise, may be judged of by this circumstance; which the Tory Leader held to be of sufficient importance to decide his non-acceptance of ministerial power. When I complained to Lord Melbourne that the lady expectant I have alluded to, took an active part against me:—his answer was,—"Not against *you*—none of them care about you: it is against *me*,— and she, in particular, has always hated me like poison."

From him I learned, that when on one occasion, whilst her Majesty's carriages were passing over the race-ground at Ascot, some of the Tory Ladies *hissed* (which caused great scandal), those ladies excused themselves by saying, they "intended no disrespect to the Queen, *for that they had hissed, not Her Majesty, but her Majesty's Minister Lord Melbourne.*" From him I learned, also, many speeches and sentiments from other ladies, which I should not else have known: and I confess that the conduct of some of these female Politicians—their capacity for bitter partisanship, and incapacity for common justice—amazed me.

I was young enough then, to expect the sympathy of all women; and I was astonished at finding ladies whose children were my contemporaries, looking upon me not only without pity, but with anger, as something that was to have wrecked the Whig Prime Minister, and had failed to accomplish that object. Fortunately for me, kindness was the rule, and harshness the exception. If misfortune taught me some bitter lessons, it also taught me the nobleness of hearts on which I had no claim. Fortunately also for me, I had true and generous sisters,—and a family whose love and protection almost annulled the bitterness of these events!

But neither family nor friends could help me to redeem those hostages—my children: and not yet seeing my way to the struggle a new law afterwards enabled me to make, I supplicated incessantly, and in vain. I thought of nothing, day or night, but my children. Lord Melbourne wrote to me, surprised at my silence after the trial; and I told him I was broken-hearted on this point, and had written to petition my husband for mercy respecting them. I wrote bitterly and despondingly; and Lord Melbourne's replies were certainly not cheering or comforting. His anger against Mr Norton for having submitted to be employed, to injure not only him but his party—*"those who are attached to me and follow my fortunes"*—was mixed with something like reproach to me, for not having more keenly and severely judged and foreseen the conduct of the husband I had toiled and asked favours for. I had not the "lover" attributed to me; but I had a friend, deeply wounded, and whom I grieved to wound; and these are his letters:

South Street, July 2nd, 1836.

Well, come what may, I will never again, from silence or any other symptom, think that you can mean anything unkind or adverse to me. I have already told you that most of the bitterness which I have felt during this affair, was upon your account... I do not think your application to Norton was judicious. From the beginning, your anxiety to prevent publicity has induced you to apply to him too much. Every communication elates him, and encourages him to persevere in his brutality. You ought to know him better than I do, and must do so. But you seem to me to be hardly aware what a *gnome* he is: how perfectly earthy and bestial. He is possessed of a devil; and that the meanest and basest fiend that disgraces the infernal regions. In my opinion he has somehow or other made this whole matter subservient to his pecuniary interest. He has got *money* by it, from — or someone else. I should feel certain of this, if it were not for his folly, which is so excessive as to render him incapable even of forwarding his own low designs.

South street, July 19th, 1836.

There is no knowing what that man may do, now that he is left to the guidance of his own feelings, and his own understanding; and to the advice of those about him. You knew the state of your own domestic affairs better than I did. I only knew what you told me; but it appeared to me, that by living

68

with him you had grown less alive to his real character by being accustomed to it, and also that you were so used to manage him and to prevent his follies, that you relied too much on being able always to do it. Recollect when you were with him, how stupidly and brutally he continually behaved; particularly, for instance, to Helen. His conduct there, always struck me as showing a violence which was likely afterwards to break out. Now that he has nobody to advise, control, or soothe him, what follies or what abominable conduct he may pursue, it is impossible to conjecture. I pity you about the children. It is most melancholy not to know where they are, or with whom.

South street, July 24, 1836.
I send you back the copies.* I agree very much in all you say in your letter. The amount of allowance makes a great difference. If you could get 300*l*. or 400*l*. (I think you ought to have the latter sum), the arrangement might do tolerably well. But they are very advantageous terms for him, and should not be agreed to, except for something approaching to an equivalent. I think he should secure your income beyond his own life, upon any property which he may have. I have never mentioned money to you, and I hardly like to do it now: your feelings have been so galled that they have naturally become very sore and sensitive, and I knew not how you might take it. I have had at times a great mind to send you some, but I feared to do so. As I trust we are now upon terms of confidential and affectionate friendship, I venture to say, that you have nothing to do but to express a wish, and it shall be instantly complied with. I miss you. I miss your society and conversation every day at the hours at which I was accustomed to enjoy them, and when you say that your place can be easily supplied, you indulge in a little vanity and self-conceit. You know well enough that there is nobody who can fill your place. I have been reading 'The Wife,' and have finished the second volume. It is full of most excellent things. 'Lionel' is too d—d a beast, and 'Mary' makes a great deal too much sacrifice for him; but it is not unnatural. Many people have acted as amiably, as romantically, and as foolishly. I think, in order to take advantage of what you have observed in other people's

* Of Mr Norton's propositions.

69

characters, you have put into his, what did not belong to it. For instance, his being so disagreeable upon the journey, calculating the currency and admiring nothing fine or beautiful either in Nature or Art, is what has struck you in others, and you have grafted it upon him; in whom, being a man of genius and feeling, it is not natural.

I saw Brinsley and his wife the other night at Lord Hertford's. I thought him rather cold. None of them seem really glad to see me, except Charlie. But there is no reason they should be. If they went upon my principle (or rather my practice) of disliking those who cause me trouble, uneasiness, vexation, without considering why they do it, they certainly would not rejoice in my presence.

You are quite right, and it shows your good sense, to bear in mind that it may be of permanent disadvantage to your children to be separated and estranged from their father's family, upon whom they must principally depend. I expect that some day or another you will have them all thrown upon you,—Adieu,

Yours, Melbourne.

South street, January 7th, 1837.
...Do you know — tells me, that from all he can hear, he believes that Norton has really got three thousand a year; and ten thousand pounds down." . . . .

South Street, January 18th, 1837.
...I have been told to-day that Norton has been trying to make a bargain to give up his office in favour of a Mr — for a thousand pounds.* It is just like him. I said to the person who gave me the intelligence, 'if you find it out, stop the bargain, and stop the appointment; but say as little as possible about it—for at least half the disgrace of the transaction will fall upon me, who appointed him.' Adieu,

Yours, Melbourne.

This, then, is the husband, who to evade a pecuniary contract, has lately subjected me to the last extreme of obloquy:

---

* At the time it was supposed that Mr Norton would be unable, after the trial, to brave public opinion by continuing to hold the place Lord Melbournę had given him.

these are the letters of the man he proceeded against, in an English Court of "Justice," for *damages*: and such are the opinions, in despite of which Mr Norton dares to revive the slur he threw upon my name in the mad vengeance of the hour,—when Sir James Graham declined his condition that if he retracted what had been said of me, we were to contradict all that was said of *him*. Lord Melbourne's letters are in themselves evidence that *I* spared Mr Norton. The man my husband accused as my lover, writes to me as to one not even thoroughly aware of that husband's mercenary nature.

> You ought to know him—but you seem to be hardly aware what a *gnome* he is. . . I only knew what you told me, but it appeared to me that by living with him you had grown less alive to his real character, by being accustomed to it. . . Recollect how he behaved, &c. . .

Phrases which prove, that to the last, *I* had spared him, to those who could serve him—and to those who could not. And if it be asked why, having spared him so long, I expose him now,—I answer that *I* am the judge,—not others,—where endurance merged in exasperation: and that the boundary line was reached, the day Mr Norton met me in the County Court; the day that, to evade a just claim, he unburied all the falsehoods of the past; endeavoured to disgrace (in 1853, as he had done in 1836) for the sake of money; and in cold blood re-published, to the grieving of my grown-up sons, the slanders which had blighted my youth in their infancy.

But for that day in the County Court, Mr Norton might have gone to his grave in seeming respectability; our history known only to a few friends. Struggle and warfare were over with me. Much of the bitterness I had felt, had faded with time; much had vanished when I recovered my sons. While that bitterness was yet fresh, and circumstances, from time to time, roused me to desire a more public justification—Lord Melbourne himself was the first to preach lessons of patience. He spoke to me of the "nine days' wonder" my story would be; of the perfect conviction of the real circumstances of my case, entertained by those whose opinion I valued; of my

71

youth, and the likelihood that in a few years I would have *"lived down"* all temporary scandal; of the embarrassment it would be to *him*—as the minister of a young unmarried Sovereign—to have such a history re-opened;—of the disloyal selfishness he conceived such a struggle on my part would evince; of the awkwardness, in particular, of any attempt to prove interference on the part of those Personages who had denied it to him; of the certainty that when the Queen was married, and the Court more established, I would find, in the earnest support of those whose faithful minister he had been, an upholding that would make me forget the disgrace I had endured in his name.

He was my friend, though not my lover; and the resolves of many an angry day and hour subsided under his influence. In later years there had been no need for such arguments for silence. I had long relinquished the idea of warfare with Mr Norton; and was quietly making the best of a bad destiny. All last winter I was residing in Italy with my two sons; occupied in completing a work to be published by Messrs Hurst and Blackett, the profits of which were devoted to the Oxford expenses of the youngest. I had just nursed him through one of those tedious Neapolitan fevers, from which he had suffered for nine weeks—I had myself been confined to my room for five weeks.

And *this* was the time chosen by Mr Norton, as husband and father, for a vain battling correspondence, compelling my return to England, to debate at law the contract I thought had been settled for life. This was the time chosen,—by subpoenaing my publishers, and claiming to reckon my literary gains as his own personal relief,—to establish his legal right to annul even the service I could render my son: and to revive libels he himself had a thousand times admitted to be false: by which he once more put me in the same position, *as to the repelling of accusation*, that I had been in when our separation took place, in 1836.

In the same position, only as to that one point. Lord Melbourne is dead; my children are grown up; I have no *second* youth, to wear away in the fond hope of "living down" Mr Norton's slanders, and making friendships and companion-

ships among my own sex without the sorrowful embarrassment of a "story" to explain.

I have no second youth, I say, to spend in a semi-
justification against these foul slanders. Therefore, once for
all, I deny them: I defy them: I disprove them: and I regret
only that I did not do, years ago, that which I do this day. As
to writing, I will never again write, while my copyrights are
held to be Mr Norton's; except on this single subject of the
state of the Laws of Protection for Women.* My youth has
gone by in struggle and vexation; much of it in bitter sorrow:
the youth of other women may be saved from such suffering
by changes in the law; and my writing on that topic, while the
law is admitted to be in a state of transition, may (without
over-rating my own power) have as much influence, as other
individuals have had in the gradual remedy of other defective laws. Such a hope has a certain degree of happiness
attached to it; even if the law be remedied too late for me
personally to profit much by the change.

I come now to the history of the contract, in the attempt to
evade which, Mr Norton revived scandal, and braved this
defence.

----

* It is my intention to follow this pamphlet by a selection of such cases as
appear to me most remarkable among decisions in the Courts of Law;
bearing on the general point of this want of protection.

V

In July 1848, my husband—who had for years allotted me precisely what he pleased—desired once more to attempt to raise the Trust-fund alluded to at page 27, that being the provision made on my marriage, for me and my sons. To raise this money, it was necessary for him to obtain my written consent. He applied to me accordingly: and I requested him, in exchange, to execute a deed of separation, and secure me an income of 600*l*. a-year (which I had been assured was the *minimum* of allowance that would have been granted, if I had been in a position to sue for alimony).

Mr Norton's reply was merely haggling as to terms: he would not give 600*l*. but he would give 500*l*.: and I must give my consent at once to raise the Trust-fund. He employed my invalid son, who had just returned on leave from Lisbon, to press this upon me; and to explain that he wanted the money immediately, to improve the estate left him by Miss Vaughan. As soon as my son interfered, I made haste to yield: I wrote to Mr Leman, who acted as solicitor for my trustees, to say that I consented to all Mr Norton proposed,—"mainly because it is intolerable to me to have my son talk over matters of this kind from his father."

But I entered on the arrangement with a distrust which subsequent events have proved to be most amply justified. I could not but remember the numerous occasions on which Mr Norton had shown that no possible reliance could be placed on his word; and I shocked Mr Leman by expectations openly and repeatedly expressed, that my husband would "cheat" me. Every one of the letters I wrote on this business, contained that truly prophetic warning.

The first hitch occurred, from Mr Norton insisting that the

deed which was to be only prospective, for *me*, should be guaranteed *retrospectively* (for a period of no less than ten years), as far as his own pecuniary advantage was concerned. This was utterly refused, and the guarantee I had named, declined to act. Mr Leman told me that, without a guarantee, the deed of separation he had prepared, would be informal. I answered that if I could not obtain a legal separation, I supposed some other kind of deed or bond could be executed; by which Mr Norton could be *bound*: and that I was to see a legal friend whom I would consult on the subject.

That legal friend was Sir Frederick Thesiger; who consented, at my earnest request, to receive Mr Norton at his chambers. Having seen him, Sir F. Thesiger wrote to me that my husband would execute a deed of separation: that he did not require guarantees, but insisted on my acceding to the condition of his retrospective advantage; which no guarantee would have acceded to, but which he declared I, personally, had promised him. Sir F. Thesiger then added,—"if he is correct in this statement—assuming the accuracy of Norton's assertion—I should venture to recommend you not to aim at any alteration of the terms, but to embrace the offer now made, of giving you the security of a deed of separation; which you have so long earnestly desired, and which I trust, will have the effect of placing you in a situation of more complete tranquillity than it has been your lot to enjoy for many years."

I did, then, what I was advised; I yielded the point of retrospective protection. I agreed, that for ten years past, and for all years to come, Mr Norton should never be troubled with any debt of mine; he agreeing in future to pay 500*l*. a year. I told Mr Leman I would be content with such a deed, signed by Mr Norton and witnessed by Sir F. Thesiger; and I left town on a visit to Lord Rutherford, the then Lord Advocate of Scotland.

The new deed was sent to Scotland for me to sign. I obeyed; and returned it by post. It never occurred to me as possible, that the instrumental was valueless. If I had thought so, I would not have gone through the ridiculous farce of signing it. I received it as the valid substitute for the unexecuted deed previously thrown aside; and as a settlement *for life*. Mr Norton, in his published letter, says that *he* knew at the time, it was invalid. If so, he was guilty of deliberate fraud: for the deed pretended to make permanent conditions, and included the contingency of his succeeding to the peerage by surviving his brother.

Even the lately disputed chance of my providing for debt beyond the allowance so secured—by literary or other resources—had been duly contemplated: Sir F. Thesiger had written to Mr Leman to guard against Mr Norton's interference in such a case, in these terms:

> I foresee the germs of endless differences if it were to be permitted. . . The spirit of the agreement I understand to be, that a certain provision should be secured to Mrs Norton; that Mr Norton should be discharged from liability for the debts, and that neither should trouble or interfere with the other.

That was also my exact understanding of the case; and Mr Norton hastened to give this earnest assurance in reply.

> I can have no wish to interfere with Mrs Norton's affairs: still less with her debts: you may bind me as stringently as you please not to interfere with her affairs. I shall pay her allowance under the deed, with the same regularity I have paid her previous allowance.

I had yet to learn how easily I had been outwitted! On the strength of the momentary value of *my* signature, Mr Norton instantly raised the money he wanted; and left me to ascertain at leisure what was the value of *his* signature.

Late in the same autumn I received news from Lisbon, that my son was considered by the physicians there to be dying: and I hurriedly proceeded to London to make preparations for going out to join him. While I was thus anxiously occupied, intelligence reached me of the dangerous illness of Lord Melbourne, and he died about a fortnight before I sailed for Portugal. I returned the ensuing year to England. My son was better, and accompanied me home: my mother was then ill, but she rallied and temporarily recovered. I went with my son to Germany and Belgium; returned again to England; and in June, 1851, my mother died.

At her death, Mr Norton inherited the life-interest of my

portion from my father, which had not been secured to me in any way: and *I* inherited,—secured to me most carefully, guarded from the rapacity of my husband, by every expression in my mother's will—an income for life of 480*l*. As soon as Mr Norton found I had this legacy, and six months before I received one farthing of it, he wrote that he could no longer pay me the sum secured (as I imagined) by the deed of agreement we had both signed; and he begged to inquire what deduction I myself would propose in my allowance,— "such deduction to commence from the time that I should receive any money under my mother's will."

I replied, that I could propose no deduction; that my mother's bequest was expressly intended as an addition, to eke out the meagre allowance he made me, and not as a substitute for such allowance; that years of litigation, dispute, and debt, the illness of my son, and my constant journeys and residences abroad in consequence of such illness, had crippled my means; that my mother's assistance was intended for me and for my sons (not for the husband who had ruined and wronged me in the days of my youth, when all the love of my family, and all the law of England, failed to protect me against him).

Mr Norton rejoined, that what I would not yield, he would take; that I should either consent to his deducting 200*l*. a year as his advantage from the 480*l*. left to me, or he would not give me anything; that I could not compel him; that as to the agreement Mr Leman had drawn up, he defied me to prove it valid, "as, by law, Man and Wife were one, and could not contract with each other; and the deed was therefore good for nothing."

I reminded him that the deed was in fact a matter of bargain, as he had expressly urged its being drawn up, in order to obtain my signature to raise the trust-money he wanted—that he had had *his* advantage, and that it was most dishonourable to evade the covenant as regarded me. Mr Norton laughed at the argument, and stood to the fact, that *in law* I could not help myself, and that the deed was valueless.

I inquired whether this was true, and was informed that Mr Norton probably *could* evade the performance of his covenant;—because the fiction of the law was, that "man and wife are one,"—and not two contracting parties—that he was not bound therefore "in law," only "in honour."

I asked what I could do under the circumstances; and was told that I might refer the creditors I could not pay to Mr Norton, and so take the chance of its being decided that he was liable, upon their suing him. I was extremely loath and unwilling to do anything. I did not believe that the deed could be proved null; or, if it could, that Mr Norton would brave the shame of publicly asserting his own signature, set to an instrument drawn up by a lawyer, under his own directions, to be worthless. A gentleman, a barrister, a magistrate: I decided in my own mind that it was *impossible*: that it was an empty treat, to induce me to share the legacy with him. I thought I would give him time. I was anxious about my second son, who had hitherto been robust, but who had been suffering a good deal. I wanted to take him away to join my other son at Naples: to have one of the gleams of peace in my tormented life, which I can at least enjoy with *them*. I could not go away, if I entered on lawsuits with Mr Norton. I therefore merely attempted to draw my usual allowance at Mr Norton's banker's according to the contract; was refused; borrowed from my own bankers, under my brother's security, a sum of money for my journey,—and left England.

I certainly gave Mr Norton ample time to consider whether he would act honestly or not; I gave him *nearly a year and a half*; from March 1852 (when he balanced my receipt of my mother's legacy by stopping my allowance), till August 1853; when I was compelled to appear in the County Court.

Neither during that time, nor since, has he paid one farthing. The *Law* has enabled him alike to defraud the dead and the living; and my mother might just as well have left the money unsecured, which he thus seized by deduction. Even the statement that he would pay a minor sum, turned out to be false; I tested it, by giving a cheque to Sir A.D. Gordon for the whole amount, and afterwards to Mr Thrupp (the creditor who lost his cause), for a small proportion of the amount; and both those cheques were returned unpaid upon my hands.

When I returned to England, I had still hoped and endeavoured to avoid any public law struggle with Mr Norton. I sent for his cousin, Mr Norton of Elton, and explained the case to him; desiring him to advise Mr Norton. I once more appealed to the wearied-out patience of Sir Frederick Thesiger. He heard me with more indulgence perhaps than I deserved, considering the irritation under which I was labouring at the position of affairs; unable to pay what I owed; frustrated in my efforts to assist either my sons or myself; and defied by Mr Norton as to the deed which I believed had closed *for life* all discussions between me and my husband.

But though Sir Frederick heard me patiently, he declined seeing Mr Norton; to whom, he said, he had become a total stranger; that it was very long since he had met him, and then not in society. I wrote, after that, to Mr Norton's own solicitor, in the forlorn hope that he might be acting against advice. I settled the first action brought against Mr Norton by promising to pay it myself, with all expenses, so soon as that should be possible. I had been subpœnaed as witness, in that and other cases; and I must observe (for many persons misunderstand this), that attendance on subpœna is compulsory, not voluntary. Mr Norton, in the subsequent case that came into court, subpœnaed a person who had been my maid; subpœnaed my bankers; compelled them to produce their books, and sent his attorney to make extracts at their bank, of all sums entered in my private account. He also subpœnaed my publishers; to compel them to declare what were the copyrights they held of me, and what sums they had paid me.

It is not to be supposed that these gentlemen had any pleasure in coming forward; or *volunteered* to uphold a defence grounded on a disgraceful quibble. They attended,—as *I* attended,—on subpœna; a legal summons, the punishment for disobeying which is a fine, or imprisonment for contempt. Subpœnaed again,—in a fresh action,—my last effort, through the solicitor, was to warn Mr Norton that I was already in debt to my banker, and could pay no other creditor. I received for answer merely that he "declined all discussion on the subject."

I then made up my mind to bear what must be borne, and went into court (as I imagined), merely to answer a few formal questions, the pain of which consisted in being obliged to prove, thus publicly, that my husband had cheated me. I expected to have to prove the contract; to prove his signature; to hear Mr Leman (who was also subpœnaed) prove the circumstances under which it was drawn out; to admit the debt; to show that I had no fund but this withheld allowance to pay it with; and then to hear it decided, either that Mr Norton *was* legally liable, or that he was *not*. I had the opinion of an able solicitor that he would be held liable. I had the opinion of the distinguished Queen's counsel who accompanied me into court, that he would not; and I was prepared for the possibility of an adverse legal decision. What I was not prepared for, was the scene that followed.

My husband had resolved how to fight this battle. He entered the court attended by counsel. (I believe counsel had not been thought necessary on the other side, which was conducted by Mr Dod, Solicitor to the Society for the Protection of Trade.) When I first saw my husband, my courage sank; the horrible strangeness of my position oppressed me with anger and shame; my heart beat; the crowd of people swam before my eyes; and the answers I had begun to make, and the declarations I had intended to struggle through, choked in my throat, which felt as if it were full of dust. It would have been well for Mr Norton if he had not then eagerly seized an imaginary advantage. He rose, gathered up his papers, and saying with a sneer—"*What does the witness say? Let her speak up; I cannot hear her;*" he came and seated himself close to me; there was only the skirting board that divided the court between us.

The witness heard *him*. That which he did still further to abash and intimidate me, had precisely the contrary effect. I knew, as I listened, that he had come with the resolution to crush me at all hazards. I felt, as I looked for an instant towards him, that he saw in me neither a woman to be spared public insult, nor a mother to be spared shameful sorrow,— but simply a claimant to be non-suited; a creditor to be evaded; a pecuniary incumbrance he was determined to be rid of. More than one of the professional gentlemen present appealed to the Judge, whether he should be "permitted" to sit where he had placed himself; but there he continued to sit; instructing his counsel in an under-tone what questions to put to me,—making written notes on the case,—and occasionally peremptorily addressing me himself. In my heart, scorn and desperation took the place of fear.

The case was a claim for 47*l*., for repairs of a little carriage in use for twelve years. I was examined; and began by stating, "that I had already stopped one case against my husband at my own expense; that I appeared in court against my will, subpœnaed by the creditor, whose account I had paid in part, and would have paid entirely, if Mr Norton had not stopped my allowance."

Mr Norton's counsel, Mr Needham, endeavoured to prevent this statement. He then cross-examined me (assisted by Mr Norton); apparently to try and prove that I was extravagant. I was questioned how many servants I kept; whether they were of an expensive class; whether I ever ventured to ask my friends to dinner; and what I needlessly spent on the education of a poor orphan girl, confided to my care by the clergyman of her parish (brother-in-law to the minister of the chapel Mr Norton and I attended in Westminster). This charity seemed especially to irritate Mr Norton. I was cross-examined about it, with the most sneering severity; it seemed as if *I* could have no right, either to the pleasures of hospitality,—or the luxury of doing good; but that every farthing not absolutely necessary to put a meal into my own mouth, ought to have been saved up and made over as a free gift to the husband who had blighted my whole existence.

In vain I assured Mr Needham that the orphan was going out to service, and that teaching her to write and read, had *not* been expensive: a charity which did not come out of the poor's-box in the magistrate's court, was incomprehensible to Mr Norton; and in daring to perform it, I had wronged and robbed him. It never seemed to occur, either to Mr Norton or to Mr Needham, that whatever I had expended was mine to expend; that I did not owe a penny I could not have paid, but for my husband's dishonesty; that whether my money was disbursed for charity—or hospitality—or even luxury (if they could have proved such a thing),—instead of being principally expended in travelling with an invalid son; and whether it was the result of legacies, or literary industry; it was my own current income; 500*l.* a year of which, being seized by Mr Norton, alone created for me any difficulty. It never seemed to occur to them, that the question was not whether my husband should provide for me; but whether he should cheat me of a *covenanted debt*, on the quibble that he could not contract with his *wife*. That if he had contracted to pay this money to the Duke of Bedford—instead of to me—he could not have disputed the debt on the ground that the Duke was already so well off, that it was unnecessary to pay him; even on proof of all the large hospitalities of Woburn.

As a matter of justice, the ground taken was simply ridiculous; and perhaps they felt it to be so; for, after vainly arguing that I ought to have spent less, (and so made a sort of nest-egg and provision against the event of my being defrauded); that ground was shifted, and the sources of my income examined into. Mr Norton, who left me, when we first parted, without any provision at all for two years,—who had insisted, at the time of our contract, on a retrospective advantage for himself, through the whole period of our separation,—and who still holds property of mine, which no referee could persuade him to give back;—took, not an average of the past, but such selected years as he pleased, from the banker's books; adding in (*as income*) the money, still unpaid, which I had borrowed of them; while Mr Needham, not being familiar perhaps with the lines,—

Lieto nido—esca dolce—aura cortese
Bramano i cigni; e non si va in Parnaso
Con le cure mordaci;

or not being of the poet's opinion as to the fate of—

Chi pur sempre
Col suo destin garrisce e col disagio—

bravely added, that I must make at least 500*l*. a year by my writings!

All this I could have borne; and almost smiled at it; false and foolish as it was; and wide of the real question, whether Mr Norton should break his written bond or not. But I was not so to be released. "The children of darkness are wiser in their generation than the children of light;" and those who had to defend fraud, felt that so it would be but ill-defended; and that the clear light would fall on a gross breach of faith. Mr Norton has had more than half a century's experience of this world; and he knew better how to evade its judgment. He knew what the introduction and revival of the old scandals about Lord Melbourne, would be worth in such a case. He knew how instantly attention would be called off the real question of our contract, to animated disputes whether the verdict given in that memorable trial had or had not been a just one; whether I was or was not a wanton; whether I had or had not done well in accepting any legacy from the defendant in that action. He knew what clouds of dust would rise with that old story, to confuse the eyes that might otherwise see clearly; and he—whose own income consisted of—

1. A place of a thousand a year given by LORD MELBOURNE:—
2. An estate in Yorkshire left him by the woman whose seizure of my children caused our last quarrel:—
3. The trust-fund from which he had borrowed, by means of my signature to the very contract disputed in Court:—
4. The portion bequeathed me by my Father:—
5. The Recordship of Guildford; a salary for sitting in judgment on other men—(!)

HE came forward in Court, to affect a scrupulous delicacy,—that the wife on whom he had closed the door of her home "with the chain across:"—whom he had prosecuted for divorce and then wooed to return to him:—whom he himself had endeavoured to make the wife of Lord Melbourne, by criminating evidence totally unfit for belief;—should accept assistance from that dead friend's family, to half the amount he himself still drew, from the place Lord Melbourne had given him!

Greater hypocrisy than the pretence, surely never existed: and a greater falsehood than that by which the pretence was supported, certainly never was told; for Mr Norton coolly asserted that he never would have made the allowance in the contract, if I had not "given him the most solemn assurance that I would receive nothing from Lord Melbourne."

I made a brief emphatic answer, to this deliberate misrepresentation. I said:—

"I stand here on my *oath*,—and I say that that is false." For a moment, I was bitterly tempted to add these further words: "Will Mr Norton also consent to be *sworn*?" But I refrained. I appealed to Mr Leman's testimony, whose evidence was taken on oath as a witness in the case—and who accordingly deposed that no such stipulation ever was made; and that he himself had drawn up the contract with all its conditions, at Mr Norton's own request. Mr Leman added—with much emphasis and feeling—that though, legally, he considered the agreement might not stand, he certainly expected it would have bound Mr Norton "*as a man of honour.*"

From the moment the questioning began about Lord Melbourne, I lost all self-possession. Not because I was ashamed of having accepted his bequest; if I had thought there was shame in it, I should not have taken it:—but because I then saw all the cruel baseness of Mr Norton's intention. All flashed upon me at once. I felt that I no longer stood in that Court to struggle for an income—but to struggle against infamy. I knew by sudden instinct, that the husband who had so often, to me and to others, asserted that the trial was the work of "Advisers" was now about to pretend he *believed* the charge brought against Lord Melbourne in 1836. The wild exasperation came over me, which seemed so inexplicable to those who did not know our real story. He, who had falsely accused me long ago,—he who had taken my young children, and let one of them die without even sending for me, till too late,—he who had embittered and clouded my whole existence,—who was now in my presence only to cheat me (as I had foretold he would do),—he was once more going to brand me before the world!

I felt giddy; the faces of the people grew indistinct; my

sentences became a confused alternation of angry loudness, and husky attempts to speak. I saw nothing—but the husband of whose mercenary nature Lord Melbourne himself had warned me I judged too leniently; nothing but *the Gnome*,— proceeding *again* to dig away, for the sake of money, what remnant of peace, happiness, and reputation, might have rested on the future years of my life. Turning up as he dug—dead sorrows, and buried shames, and miserable recollections—and careless who was hurt by them, so long as he evaded payment of a disputed annuity, and stamped his own signature as worthless!

I tried, at first confusedly enough (as the broken sentences in the reports showed), but afterwards as connectedly as I could, to explain that Lord Melbourne had left me nothing in his will; that I believed he could not, his property being strictly entailed; that I had never been his mistress; that I was young enough, and more than young enough, to be his daughter, and that he had never treated me otherwise than as a friend: that the trial of 1836 was based on a false accusation; and that Lord Melbourne had given his word of honour when living, to that effect: that, dying, he had left nothing but a letter solemnly repeating that denial; recommending me to the generosity of his brother, and stating the amount of provision he wished made for me: that his brother and his sister had abided by and fulfilled his intentions, because his memory was dear to them; and none but my husband had ever accused him of baseness. That I received what he had wished me to receive, but that *I* held no legal security to oblige any one to pay it; not even such a security as the contract Mr Norton had mocked me with; drawn up by a lawyer and signed by that lawyer and my husband": that Lord Melbourne had relied on his family showing me this kindness after he was gone, on account of the disgrace and misery I had most unjustly endured in his name; and that they had done so.

And certainly (if I may add to the acknowledgment of that kindness, one selfish comment), I think never woman had fairer claim on kindness; for if it had not been for the scheme to oust Lord Melbourne as Minister, my quarrel with my husband would have been arranged—as other disputes had been; Mr Norton having already owned to Sir James Graham, that he was ready, conditionally, to retract what he had said against me. And if it had not been for Lord Melbourne's position afterwards, as Minister,—and above all, the embarrassment of his being Minister to a young Queen, at the time when I was most eager to institute some suit against Mr Norton that might lead to my public justification,—I could long ago have made my husband's weapons of slander recoil upon himself, as I do this day; and the trial of 1836 would have received that explanation which even *now* I have given within the limits of a certain discretion. Lord Melbourne repeatedly thanked me, for not moving in this matter; and for him, and for his interests, I bore much which I certainly need not have borne.

When Mr Norton's counsel had received answers to the questions he put, relative to the supposed bequest, he paused; and then proceeded to cross-examine me, as though he believed I had perjured myself. This gentleman's manner of questioning, was so insolent and offensive, that at one time Mr Hayward appealed to the Judge on my behalf; and I was obliged to remind him that I was answering him "upon oath." He insisted that there *had* been some stipulation with Mr Norton about his money. He endeavoured to show (in spite of my denials), that it *was* secured, and *was* a legacy. He said—as if to confound me by proof—"You received a certain sum in January, and an equal sum in July. Do you not know that the difference between those two sums and the income Lord Melbourne left you, is made up by the Legacy Duty?"

I said I did not know what the differnce was made up by; all I knew was, that the payment depended on the pleasure (or the "*charity*," if he pleased) of Lady Palmerston; and *not* on legal securities. Mr Leman then explained that the difference was made up by the Income Tax.

In proportion as Mr Needham was baffled in what he had intended to prove, he became irritated and uncivil: he said to me in so many words, speaking of Mr Norton,—"You know you ran away from him," and, at another time, "It is not *his* fault you stand in the degraded position you do." And it was against the insult of this phrase, that Mr Hayward rose and appealed.

The feeling in Court began to show itself in a strong and obvious sympathy for me; and the case became more like a vehement debate than a judicial inquiry. Mr Needham lost even the form and pretence of adhering to the subject before the Court (*i.e.* the debt and contract), and put question after question about Lord Melbourne; what had become of his letters—what had occurred with respect to him in 1836? Whether I had got my maid's husband appointed a police usher through Lord Melbourne (as if that was a wrong); and when I said "No," again adopted the manner of disbelieving my reply.

In utter exasperation, I alluded to the circumstances of the attempted divorce; to the letters signed Greenacre &c.; and said—"If Mr Norton thought me unfaithful to him, why did he write and adjure me to return?" Mr Needham replied,— "Pray confine yourself to my questions;" and I retorted, "I told you to beware of your questions if you were afraid of my answers: for seventeen years I have concealed these matters, and *you* force their revelation this day."

I then added, that it was quite unnecessary to continue the debate about my means; that now that I knew the contract could be disputed, and I and my creditors defrauded, I should alter the scale of my expenses to a narrower economy. Mr Dod examined me, to show that the annuity from my mother was the real occasion of Mr Norton's breach of contract: Mr Leman was examined to prove that there had been no condition whatever, respecting Lord Melbourne, either written or verbal: and the Judge decided (not on the validity of the contract, but on the point that the allowance had not been stopped when this particular debt was incurred), that the creditor should be nonsuited. Mr Norton then vehemently addressed me—the Judge—the reporters for the press: he said I had told the grossest falsehoods (I having been examined on oath): that he only regretted he had no opportunity at present—that he hoped at some future opportunity, to "give the contradiction that from his heart and soul he could give." He moved still nearer to me; clenched his hand, and spoke in a threatening manner; but the groaning, and utter confusion in Court made it difficult, even for me, to gather exactly what his threats were, except that they had reference to the hope of some fresh occasion for debate. The Judge ordered the Court to be cleared, and the next cause called on: and so ended this disgraceful scene.

In Mr Norton's memorable letter to the "Times" (which I shall presently give), he sneers at the evidence of my distress and agitation that day, as a piece of "acting." Having himself experienced no touch of pity, tenderness, or honourable sense of degradation,—the reverse was a mystery he could not solve. It could only be acting. What was there to feel any distress about? What?

In the sudden echo of shame-struck and grieving days of the trial, long ago (when at least life lay before me); and in the consciousness that I had, as I have said, no second youth to wear away in a sort of struggling hope; but that all was now over *for ever*. In the memory of the frank friend, whose attempt to aid me was made the vile pretence of this dispute: who was dead: who could no longer give his word of honour in my defence, nor listen patiently to my complaining, and speak cheerful prophecies of my "living down" slander. In the recollections knitted with the time of his death: the voyage to Lisbon: the lonesome residence there, away from all friends: the refusal of my husband, even when I was returning with a son pronounced dying by the Portugese physicians, to bear *his* share in any unusual expense,—to pay his passage home, or even to refund a trifling debt borrowed of the British Minister. What was there in all this? and yet this was the time when Lord Melbourne's brother placed that legacy to my account! truly I was not thinking then of proud and fastidious scruples: I was thinking where we should have to go next: to Madeira, or the Cape of Good Hope; to see my son die where my father had died. I had already lost my uncle, who was generous to me, and with whom I had found a home after the trial: the literary tasks, on which so much stress was laid by Mr Norton's counsel, were utterly suspended: and I was simply glad—(let those sneer at it who

89

please)—that with such a husband, and such a destiny of never-ending troubles, the family of the man in whose name I had suffered so much, were willing to prove, not for my sake but for his, that his kindness to me outlived him.

In the consciousness, then, of being made once more a subject of hateful annoyance to that family, to whom I would fain have been welcome; and especially of pain to Lord Melbourne's sister, who at the very time Mr Norton was bandying questions about her fulfilment of his privately expressed wishes,—and making her adherence to them a theme for public scandal,—was in deep mourning for the last of her three brothers.

And a more tender, affectionate, and devoted, sister and friend, I verily believe no brothers ever had.

In meeting the husband from whom I was separated, as a *foe*, in open Court; he himself a barrister, instructing counsel before my face, how best to attack me; I having no counsel, and never having stood in a Court of Justice before; in hearing my husband hooted and groaned at by the crowd, when the case was explained; in hearing his assertion respecting his breach of contract proved *false*, by evidence tendered on oath; in hearing the solicitor to my trustees tell *him*,—a magistrate, a peer's brother,—the father of my sons,—that it was expected the signed contract would have bound him "as a man of honour;" or, in other words, that he was *not* a man of honour; and seeing him shrink silently, unable to repel this insult; in the stinging, maddening thought of what the report of that morning's unexpected flood of slander would be to my *sons*; whose first information of it would probably be (as indeed it was), from the English newspapers; they being then at Naples:—and in the knowledge of what it must be to all my own family, who had upheld me so earnestly through previous defamation and sorrow—

In the regret (too late regret!) that I had not borrowed money from any friend who would lend it, to pay my creditors; and allowed Mr Norton to seize all he coveted; instead of believing that the fear of exposure would prevent his disputing the contract (as it prevented his disputing my petition under the Infant Custody Bill), and that at the eleventh

90

hour he would decently pay what as a "Man of Honour" he was bound to pay—so that I should not have to come into Court at all—

In the grating, hopeless knowledge, that every fraction of all he had ever said in his moods of desire for reconciliation, was false as the rest: and that there he sate, who had written me such caressing letters,—making notes of accusation; and repeating,—for the sake of money,—slanders he had solemnly declared he did not believe, sixteen years before—

In the horrible gulf of difference, between reading the evidence of a drunken groom, in those vanished miserable times, and in hearing my own husband now echo that groom's voice;—seeing him cower, like that groom, before the proof of truth, and the jeers of the crowd;—knowing he yet hoped, like that groom, that his slander would be stronger than my struggle against it—

In the bitter thought, that I might (the destiny is not so rare among women) I *might* have been married to some one with the heart of a man, and the mind of a gentleman, who would have loved and sheltered me;—or even if he had quarrelled with me, would have made warfare *decent*;—instead of standing, as I did that day, shamed and slandered *by my husband in person*,—before a wondering, curious crowd—who no doubt, many of them, blessed Heaven, that their humbler homes were more "respectable" than that of this Lord's brother, and his insulted wife—

In the insolence of the cross-examining counsel; accustomed as I have ever been to a most indulgent and high-bred courtesy, from men immeasurably Mr Needham's superiors; and to insult from *none*; except from those who have been fee'd for the task by the husband who swore at God's altar to "*protect me*"—

In all this, what was there to excite—to grieve—to render desperate—to wring the heart, and bewilder the brain?

Nothing. It could only be *acting*.

So Mr Norton affirmed. Whether his counsel also was of that opinion, I do not know; but it is impossible for me to quit this part of my subject, without making some brief comments on what is termed the "license of the Bar."

91

In this same year of 1853, much scandal was excited by a case in which a barrister having to defend a man for burglariously entering a house by night, suggested in behalf of his burglar, that he might perhaps have had a love-appointment with the lady of the house! This extraordinary insult being complained of the barrister pleaded "licence of the Bar."* Mr Needham copied this gentleman's fashion of defence; and laboured hard to prove it was somehow my fault and my shame, that I had been cheated. When the case was over, he tendered me a sort of apology, saying, that "however impertinent I might consider his questions, they were within the limit of his legal instructions."

Those instructions proceeding from Mr Norton, I am willing to believe the truth of this assertion: but I will venture to tell Mr Needham, that a lawyer who has the soul of a gentleman, does not consider he pawns it for the day, when he takes his barrister's fee; or that donning his wig and gown, transforms him into a creature taken out hunting in a leash, to let slip upon the prey at the will of his employer. Refinement of

---

* The instance here referred to, is a remarkable illustration of what lawyers think permitted to them as advocates. I give the case from a brief note in one of the papers of the day:—"THE MORALITY OF THE BAR.—In the Central Criminal Court, on Monday, a man named John Richards, aged twenty-two, was indicted for feloniously breaking and entering the dwelling-house of John Crossley, with intent to steal his goods. The prisoner was seen to loiter about the house, and to open the door with a latch-key. An alarm was instantly given, so that he had no opportunity to take anything; and he was tracked and found in the bedroom of a lady-lodger. On being asked to account for his being in the house, he said that he expected to meet a gentleman. Mr Sleigh [we quote the words of the report], in his address to the jury for the prisoner, insinuated that he had gone into the room by appointment *with the lady who was the occupier of it*; and on that ground he called upon them to acquit him. The Recorder, in his charge, told the jury that there did not appear in evidence the slightest foundation for such an imputation; and the verdict of guilty was at once pronounced. A certificate of a former conviction for felony was then put in; whereon Mr Sleigh intimated that, if he had been aware of the existence of a previous conviction, he should not have suggested the defence he did to the jury. The Recorder expressed his opinion that *the defence was most unjustifiable*. The prisoner said 'it was not suggested in his brief.' Mr Sleigh admitted that the defence was not suggested to him in his brief, but said that it occurred to him as a legitimate one to offer to the jury upon the facts of the case!"

92

manner depends upon the society a man happens to live in; but refinement of mind depends on those high instincts of honour and delicacy which belong to no class, but to the truest nobility of nature. The hired soldier is bound to draw his sword against his foe, but no man can compel him to mangle the wounded. The "hired Masters of the Tongue-fence"—as Milton calls lawyers—should do their trade more nobly. I depended that day, as to the legal decision, on a legal quibble: but for the *manner* in which that quibble was sustained, I depended on the courtesy of the English Bar; in the person of whoever represented it for the hour; I hold therefore, that Mr Needham insulted, not me, but his brethren of the bar, and the brilliant profession to which he belongs (a profession which has produced more distinguished men than any other in England),—when, by his lame apology, he implied, that while he pleaded as a lawyer, he was obliged to forget he was a gentleman.

VI

After the proceedings were ended; and when we were discussing the extraordinary defence falsely set up; it was suggested to me, that the comparative dates of Lord Melbourne's death, and the drawing up of the contract, would prove at once the impossibility of what Mr Norton had asserted. I regretted that I had not had those dates in Court: and after reading the evidence next morning, I addressed the following letter to the papers:

To the Editor,
Sir,—I ask your patience for this letter, in consequence of the unexpected falsehood by which Mr Norton yesterday upheld his non-liability to my creditors in the County Court. Mr Norton there declared that his stipulation with me was, that he should be liable only "If I received no aid from the late Lord Melbourne's family."
The solicitor who drew up the agreement contradicted him on oath—on oath he stated that there was no such stipulation.
I contradict him on facts, which are stronger than oaths. Our agreement was signed in September, 1848, and Lord Melbourne was then still alive; therefore it is *impossible* that any stipulation should have been made as to his supposed bequests. To save himself from the payment of $500 a year— due to my creditors on a formal covenant—Mr Norton has uttered this falsehood, and raked up, from the ashes of the past, an old refuted slander, on which, for two hours yesterday, he himself in person, and the counsel he employed, examined and cross-examined me, on topics which had nothing to do with the case, but which were to imply degradation and shame!
Once for all, I did not part from my husband on Lord Melbourne's account; nor had Lord Melbourne anything whatever to do with our quarrel. I parted from Mr Norton because

I persisted in an intention to take my children to my brother's house, where my husband, on account of his own conduct, was not received. My husband sent my children to a woman with whom he was intimate, and who has since left him an estate in Yorkshire; and we separated upon that. I had no other ground of dispute with my husband. The slanders respecting Lord Melbourne were an after-thought.

So it was yesterday. Mr Norton did not make any such stipulation with me as he says he did. There was then no question of bequests from Lord Melbourne—for Lord Melbourne was not dead. Mr Norton broke his covenant, according to his own letter, because my mother left me an annuity. There is not a syllable in his letter of any other cause. He introduced Lord Melbourne's name yesterday to pain and insult me, and also to draw off public attention from the fact of the positive fraud committed on my creditors by his withholding the sum due to them. The year after the action against Lord Melbourne, he besought my return home, and my forgiveness, in the most endearing terms. He threw the blame of the trial on Lord Grantley, Lord Wynford, and the political party to which they belonged. If he believed the slander, he was base to write caressing letters to persuade me to return to him; if (as is the fact) he did *not* believe that slander, he is doubly base to invoke the name of the dead against the mother of his grown-up sons, in a public court, by way of excusing his violation of a solemn covenant.

All this, though it is life and death to me, may not interest the public. But what *does* interest the public is the state of the law. By the law as it stands, if Mr Norton can evade his covenant (as he does, by stating that it is null because it was a contract with *me*, and "a man cannot contract with his own wife") he can defraud the creditor, for if a creditor sues me, I have only to plead "coverture," plead that I am a married woman, and the creditor who could not recover against Mr Norton is equally unable to recover against me. Between the facts, that because I am Mr Norton's wife *he* can cheat me, and because I am Mr Norton's wife I can cheat others, the tradesmen who have supplied me would (by the law of England) utterly lose their money.* This *does* interest the public,

* A case in point has been lately decided; January 21, 1854, in the Court of Exchequer. A married woman, representing herself to be single, executed a promissory note for one Brassey, and thereby induced the Liverpool Adel-

and is a state of the law which certainly requires amending. The case yesterday, was technically decided on this point, viz., that at the time this particular bill was incurred, the allowance had not been stopped. The validity of the covenant Mr Norton is attempting to break was not called in question; and it does interest the public and the bar—whether it *can* be called in question—whether, if not a contract with me, is not a contract with my creditors—a written and stamped agreement with *them*, made by a magistrate and barrister; because, as I have stated, if it is not a valid contract, the creditor may be utterly cheated of his money—if (which God forbid), copying the example of Mr Norton, I also should fling off, by quibble of the law, my personal liability.

Mr Norton, after a pause of a day or two, published an "answer" of extraordinary length; premising, especially, that he did so—less in his private, than his public capacity; his private character being "safe in the hands of those who knew him.") That it was, in short, as the person appointed—by Lord Melbourne—to the Metropolitan Magistracy, that he proceeded to accuse Lord Melbourne (now dead, and unable to contradict him) of every degree of turpitude; from the seduction of his wife, to the appointing of a Treasury Messenger "as a reward" for treacherously purloining his own compromising and inculpating letters from Mr Norton's house.

But I will permit Mr Norton to speak for himself; and give his letter, as he published it. He says, then:—

It is as a *Magistrate*—an administrator of Justice (according to my ability)—that I come forward in the present matter with a plain statement of facts, to prove that I have striven to be as just in my private affairs as it is my aim and desire to be

---

phi Loan Association to lend him 30*l*. It was ruled by the Chief Baron, that as a married woman could not bind herself by a contract, no action could lie against her, or her husband, for the breach of such contract; nor could she, or her husband, be sued for the fraud on the association. How are the lenders to recover their money?

in my public capacity! It is with pain that I feel myself compelled to break the silence which the forebearance of seventeen long years has made habitual to me; but I feel I must now speak out, and that it would be treason to my character and fair fame to leave all these accusations unanswered. I was subpœnaed on Thursday last by the Messrs. Thrupp, and when Mrs Norton had concluded her evidence, I begged their solicitor to call me as a witness. He refused me that favour, and, as the advocate of my opponent, I cannot quarrel with his discretion; and perhaps it was better that the opportunity was not afforded me, for in the distraction of the moment I might have been tempted to reveal matters with which, for the happiness of others, it is much better the public should remain unacquainted. My counsel was refused, even by statement, to contradict the gross falsehoods which had been most illegally and improperly introduced into the case. The question was one simply of liability; and the moment that Mrs Norton admitted she was living apart from me by her own wish (and which she did so admit at the begining of her examination), there was an end of the case, and all proceedings should have terminated. Unhappily, the judge, and every one engaged for or against her in the cause, seemed overpowered by Mrs Norton's demeanour; and those who had a turn for the drama (of whom, unfortunately, my own solicitor was one), were suspended in breathless, helpless inaction. None who witnessed that scene can forget it to their lives' end—all must remember it as the most splendid piece of *acting* ever exhibited; however much the sober mind of England must revolt against the disgrace of a court of justice being turned into the stage of Drury-lane.

My denials shall be as few as possible and as brief.

First. The agreement, or rather the memorandum, of 1848 was not a binding one. Mrs Norton knew this as well as I did—at least, her own solicitor told me it was not at the time we signed it; moreover, she did try then to make the contemplated arrangement between us a binding document, by finding trustees, but failed to do so, as not one of her relations or friends would become her surety.

One of Mrs Norton's stipulations in the memorandum was not observed from the very first, for constant applications have been made to my solicitor and myself for payment of her debts. Nevertheless, had our relative circumstances remained as they were when we entered into it, I should have continued

98

to pay her $500 per annum. She was quite correct in court when she swore that her non-reception of the annuity from Lord Melbourne formed no part of the conditions upon which that agreement was come to. I never said it did. Lord Melbourne was then alive, and I had no tangible grounds for then raising the question; but some short time afterwards I was informed by a person, who shall be nameless, after the oath that was given on Thursday (but I speak from recollection only, not having refreshed my memory with the correspondence which passed between us at the time) that Lord Melbourne had left a sealed letter for his brother, stating that he (Lord Melbourne) might have given her an annuity upon the lands he had himself acquired, but that he preferred leaving it to the convenience of his brother to secure her in an annuity of $600 per annum, of some other sum, and he (the person alluded to) added, that I might depend on this information, as he had it from one of the executors. I was surprised and disgusted, and immediately wrote to Mrs Norton to inquire if she did receive that annuity. Her answer was emphatically in the negative, and at that period she spoke the truth; for I afterwards was informed that a difference had arisen between herself and the representatives of Lord Melbourne as to giving up his letters, and which letters, as I was informed, it was insisted should be given up before the annuity was granted.

I think it was not till the close of 1851, or in 1852, that I was informed that she certainly did receive the annuity, when I again required her written denial of the fact. She answered by saying that I insulted her by repeating the question; but, not being quite satisfied with the reply, I requested my son Fletcher to speak to her on the subject, and assure her that no insult was intended by the question, and that I insisted on an explicit answer to it.

She then did explicitly assure my son that she received no annuity of any kind from Lord Melbourne, and Fletcher added, from himself, that he was fully persuaded, from her manner and words, as to the truth of her assertion. This must have been in 1852, or in this very year. Judge then, of my *surprise*, when my solicitor ascertained, *only two or three weeks ago*, that she had been in the receipt of that annuity ever since 1849! I was not permitted at the trial to enter into any explanation whatever on this or any other point; but the few and hurried observations I did make, had reference to the continuance of my allowance to her one hour, after such a fact had been clearly brought to my knowledge. The confusion that prevailed at the trial rendered it impossible for me even to explain the matter to my counsel; and hence arose that part of the cross-examination, which implied that a pledge had been given before the signing of the memorandum.

It is true, that in 1837 we contemplated a re-union. She had assured me that she had taken the sacrament in attestation of her innocence of all criminality; that assurance and other circumstances induced me to believe her innocent of the last offence; but of the impropriety of her conduct and total disregard of outward appearance, by which alone society can form its opinion, no one who moved in our circle could doubt. My own conduct, I admit, at that time was weak and vacillating in the extreme. I had loved her to madness for three or four years before I married her, and after we were united she had all power over me. But all idea of re-union was abruptly broken off when certain tidings reached me of her séjour in the Isle of Wight. From that moment my honour was outraged, and our re-union rendered impossible. Judge, then, of my surprise within the last three or four years to receive hints from her as to our living again together: one of these I can distinctly remember. My son Fletcher was seriously ill at her house, and I went there to see him. I was remarking to him that I was about taking a new lease of my house, when she said, "What nonsense, when there's a room for you here." Would any one believe that in 1849 such a proposal could have come from the person who, on Thursday last, denounced me in the way she did?

But to return to our money differences. When we first separated I divided my income—then only 800*l.* or 900*l.* per annum, into three portions. One I paid into Messrs Ranson's for her support, the second I allotted for payment of our debts, and the third for the three children and myself; and, after paying their expenses, I had not more than 5*s.* per day for myself to live upon in town, having to attend to my police court. In 1838, my cousins, Mr Vaughan and his sister, fulfilled their deceased mother's wishes, by leaving me their Yorkshire estates, and I immediately increased Mrs Norton's allowance to 400*l.* per annum, exclusive of her pension. She declined at first receiving it; she preferred furnishing houses and disposing of them, and leaving the tradesmen to bring their action in the superior courts. At least thirty suits were instituted against me for debts of her contracting. In two cases only were the opinions of juries taken, and in both the verdicts were for me.*

But the expense of defending myself against such ruination was very heavy; and I had to borrow, if I recollect, 5,000*l.* or 6,000*l.* in Scotland and elsewhere to meet it. In 1848 it was suggested that it would be a saving of interest to borrow that money of the trustees out of my patrimony, and notice was given to the bondholders in Scotland that they would be paid at a certain time. Mr Leman prepared the mortgage deed for the trustees over my Yorkshire estates; but after the preparation of the mortgage had proceeded nearly to completion, and much expence incurred therein, he told me he had discovered, what he ought from the first to have known—that the trustees could not lend the trust-money without the permission of Mrs Norton and myself in writing, and he informed me, further, that she would not give her permission, unless I consented to give her an addition of 100*l.* to her allowance, making it 500*l.* instead of 400*l.* I was driven into a corner by this unexpected discovery, and I had to submit to the addition. In 1851, my younger son's expenses at Oxford increasing, and my own expenses in Yorkshire being greater to keep up the rents in the then depressed state of agriculture, I learnt that Mrs Norton had been left 500*l.* per annum by her mother, from whom I was not aware that she had any expectations. I then proposed to her a reduction of her allowance, which she would not accede to; and, after she had received her mother's legacy and for some time enjoyed it, I did reduce it to 300*l.* per annum, but which she has never accepted.

Now, as to her access to the three children. My first idea upon her leaving me, was to place them with herself, and I never denied her reasonable access to them; but she made three different attempts to carry them off—from Storey's gate, from Ryde, and from Wonersh; and she resolutely refused to guarantee me against similar attempts, her object evidently being by every means and pretence to excite public sympathy on the subject of the children, and for which I gave her no grounds. I was responsible for their maintenance and education, and I dreaded her intention of taking them abroad. I therefore ultimately sent them to my sister's, Lady Menzies, in Scotland, providing them with a tutor; they were thence

---

* See the strange boast in a subsequent letter, of the rejection of Sir John Bayley's evidence by Lord Abinger, which produced this result.

sent to Dr Buckland, at Laleham; thence the two eldest went to Eton; and the poor youngest died of lock-jaw, resulting from a mere scratch on the bone of his elbow by a fall from his pony. He died at Kettlethorp, my place in Yorkshire, and the moment the first symptoms of lock-jaw and of danger were discovered, I sent immediately for Mrs Norton, but she arrived not until after he had expired.

Both my elder sons stayed some years at Eton, and then Fletcher went to Lisbon as attaché, with an outfit that cost me upwards of 400*l.* and an allowance of 300*l.* per annum, which he enjoys up to this moment. Fletcher was ill at Lisbon, and Mrs Norton took Brinsley out there, removing him from Eton against he advice of Mr Coleridge, his tutor, and myself. I had much difficulty in getting him back to England, when I placed him with a private tutor, Mr Heatly, to whom I paid 200*l.* per annum to prepare him for college. He then went to University College, Oxford, and, although I gave him an outfit, and allowed him 250*l.* per annum, the utmost sum Dr Plumtre advised, and which sum was afterwards increased, he got into such difficulties that he is living abroad, and I am now at an expense for his support and maintenance there. In addition to these allowances, I have sent money at various times to Lisbon, Germany, and Italy, for the support of my sons. My house has always been open to receive them; and they have not unfrequently availed themselves of it as a home. During their whole lives I have paid for their clothing, schooling, and support, with the exception of their viands at those periods when they have lived with their mother, and it was one of my many astonishments on Thursday to hear her unblushingly state that all I had done for them was to pay for their education.

The history of the action against Lord Melbourne was shortly this:—I had observed from the time of their close intimacy, Mrs Norton had taken less interest in our then only child and in myself. On one occasion, I had seen her arm round his neck, and when I remonstrated with her, she said, "Well, and what if I had my Melly round the neck—what was it?" I was jealous, and mentioned the subject to Mrs Sheridan, who quite lulled my suspicion by telling me that he had been her father's friend, and other circumstances; and on the morning of the 30th of March, 1835, I had no suspicion whatever that their intimacy was anything more than Platonic. On that morning Mrs Norton left her home, leaving her letter-bureau, by accident, open, and I saw piles of Lord Melbourne's letters lying in it. She never showed me his letters, saying letters were not meant for two; and, knowing her particularly about her letters, without looking at one, I locked the door of the room in which they were, and giving my servant, Fitness, the key, gave him the most positive orders that no one should enter the room until Mrs Norton returned, in order that she might see that they were untouched, and just as she had left them. I then took my children to the country, but the next day was surprised to receive a letter from Fitness, to say that Mr Charles Sheridan, Mrs Norton's brother, had come at six o'clock in the morning, and asked for some papers out of the bureau for a publication Mrs Norton was then engaged on, and that he had permitted him to take them.

I came to town immediately, and found that the bureau had been emptied of its contents. I then for the first time suspected something wrong. I searched about, and found a small writing-desk in the room which had escaped observation. I opened it, and found the two or three letters of Lord Melbourne which were produced at the trial, and one or two letters and papers of a more suspicious character written by a gentleman at Eastbourne. I scolded Fitness for his disobedience of orders. He said he had told Mr Charles Sheridan of the strict orders I had given him; but Mr Charles Sheridan said Mrs Norton must have her writings for the publication she was then engaged on, and he then allowed him to go into the room and take them away. He also admitted that money had been promised, to induce him to give them up; and I well remember my observation, that he had better give it to a hospital or some charity, for it would never do him good.

Mr Charles Sheridan was subpœnaed at the trial to prove the abstraction of the letters; and why he was not called I never knew.*

This very Fitness soon afterwards was appointed a messenger at the Treasury as a *reward* for his treachery. (!)

Sir W. Follett was a stranger to me; but in my emergency I showed the documents found in the writing-desk to him, and by *his* advice I was guided in all that followed. By *his* direction inquiries were first made respecting the gentleman who

---

* He was not called, because he could have proved this plausible story to be a most wicked fabrication. No one was called who could have proved the *truth*.

103

had occasioned our immediate quarrel, and who had been seen with her that morning, and then respecting one or two others, but no sufficient evidence was found. Then a negotiation for a separation was entered upon; and it was not for some weeks that the evidence of a man that had been in my service some time previous came to my knowledge. That evidence was discarded at the trial; but circumstances have since come to my knowledge which compel me to believe that he was the witness of *truth*. It suited the defendant's counsel in that action to give it a political complexion; but I solemnly declare, upon my honour, that not a single person of the Tory or any other party persuaded me to bring it; and no communication whatever had I with Lord Wynford or any other person connected with politics about it until after the trial was over. Mr Currie, my solicitor for the action, will vouch for this; and he is also aware of certain solicitations made by both parties in politics that I would not proceed with the action; he is aware how my witnesses were molested and tampered with in town, and that it was at their own request some of them were sent to the country, where they were nevertheless followed and persecuted.

I find, from the report, that Mrs Norton said on Thursday that I had claimed the copyrights of her works from her publishers; this statement I have to deny in the most distinct and emphatic terms. I have never, directly or indirectly, made any claim whatever to her copyrights, the benefit of which she has always been allowed by me to enjoy without let or hindrance; and, until I was preparing for this trial, I never even enquired as to the amount of them. What did occur with regard to her copyrights was, that my solicitor, to prove that her income has exceeded 1,500*l.* per annum, did institute an inquiry among her publishers, several of whom were subpœnaed to attend. I heard her refer to her copyrights, but did not hear her use the word "claim." I thought she referred to the inquiries my solicitor had made, and consequently used the words, "My solicitor did." Had the word "claimed" actually reached my ears, I should have doubted their accuracy in conveying to my mind so great a falsehood.

A most absurd and false impression was given by Mrs Norton as to my signature of "Greenacre." The joke involved in such a signature was but a poor one; but she forgets to state that it originated with herself, by her adopting, in her letters to me, the name of "Hannah Brown." With regard to another matter, Mrs Norton, in her letter to the "Times," uses these words:—"Because as I have stated, if it is not a valid contract, the creditor may be utterly cheated of his money, if (which God forbid!) I should copy Mr Norton, and also fling off, by a quibble of the law, my liability to them." Mrs Norton, in this quotation, refers to the plea of her coverture; now it so happens that within the last few weeks a poor man, Peter Dooladdy, came to and showed me a notice that he had received from the Westminster County Court, informing him that Mrs Norton would plead coverture in an action which he had there brought against her for wages due to him, and I understood that she has given a similar notice to several others of her creditors.

Lord Melbourne promised me the appointment of police magistrate before he visited at our house, or before, I believe, he even knew Mrs Norton (!)

Lord Eldon had appointed me Commissioner of Bankrupts in 1827, and when such appointment was abolished by the construction of the Bankruptcy Court in 1830 or 1831, I considered that I had some claim on the Home Secretary, having received no compensation for the loss of my situation. I must add, the acceptance of the police magistracy necessarily involved the relinquishment of my profession.

Mr Trail, the receiver of my rents, proved on Thursday that my income from every source did not average 2,400l. per year.

It is true, therefore, that the agreement of 1848, to allow 500l. a year was not conditioned upon the relinquishment of an allowance from Lord Melbourne's estate. It is not true that I ever said or suggested the contrary. It is true that after Lord Melbourne's death, and when I was informed of such an allowance, I required Mrs Norton's solemn assurance that she had never received, and would not receive, an income from such a source; that at one time that solemn assurance was given; that at another the bare suggestion that any such benefaction from Lord Melbourne had been accepted was treated as an insult, and that nevertheless, upon obtaining access to her bankers' books, I ascertained that she had actually received that allowance from Lord Melbourne's estate from 1849.

It is not true that I refused to perform the agreement of 1848, because it was made between man and wife; but it is true, that the agreement, having been of a temporary and not of a permanent nature, and the amount allowed under it being necessarily dependent upon the amounts of our respective incomes, I did, in 1851, upon Mrs Norton's income being increased by 500*l*. a year upon her mother's death, while mine was, from various causes, diminished, propose to reduce the 500*l*. to 300, which I was afterwards willing to increase to 400*l*.

It is also true, that down to March in the last year (1852), since when, and from the year previous, the amount of the allowances has been the subject of discussion, I allowed to Mrs Norton the undiminished sum of 500*l*. a year; that, consequently, for several years she has,—and that even by her own admission—been in the receipt of an income of at least 1,500*l*. a year and always has had an income far larger in proportion than mine; and yet she has incessantly contracted debts with numerous honest creditors, very many of whom are at this moment unpaid, and instead of applying her abundant means to the payment of these debts, has driven the creditors to resort to me, oppressing me with litigation* and costs, and impairing my already crippled means, which should have been applied to the maintenance of myself and my two sons, both of them just entering life. It is under these circumstances that I ask, on whom it is that the coarse and serious charge of cheating creditors may be truly made?

I am, Sir, your obedient, humble servant,
10, Wilton place, Aug. 23.   G.C. Norton.

The first public notice of this astonishing series of fabrications, came from Mr Leman. Having pointed out the utter inaccuracy of the portion that came within his own knowledge, namely the drawing up of the contract, he very courteously proposed that it should be corrected by Mr Norton himself. That not being complied with, Mr Leman addressed the editor of the "Times,"—briefly stating, that with the exception that he had prepared the mortgage,—"the entire paragraph was untrue." Mr Norton's solicitor having attempted some explanation in reply, Mr Leman published a complete statement of the drawing out of the contract, together with the contract itself; and concluded his letter by requesting those who might read it, to decide for themselves,

* The litigation being solely and entirely caused, by Mr Norton's refusal to be bound by his own signature to be a legal document.

whether the entire paragraph, with the exception made, was or was not "untrue."

It was then my turn to repel the accusations published by my husband. I might have answered, (as my brother's solicitor had answered Mr Norton's advertisement in 1837;) "the *whole* of it is false"; for, to contradict every falsehood, would have been to contradict every line. I left much unnoticed. My object was to keep clearly and steadily to this broad general contradiction:—that neither our quarrel in 1836 nor our dispute in 1854, had anything whatever to do with Lord Melbourne.

I left unheeded, then, the cold and stupid sneer which stamped my distress in the county court as "acting"; and the observations (made in a like spirit) as to my grief at first parting with my children, being "a pretence to excite public sympathy;" though in the very same sentence, Mr Norton relates the lamentable death of the youngest under circumstances that might well wring the hardest hearts.

I left unnoticed the whole fable of the seizure of Lord Melbourne's letters, and the wicked inventions respecting my Mother and Brother, both deceased. I left to the common sense of those who might read Mr Norton's letter, very many of his manifest self-contradictions; such as calling on his readers to "judge of his surprise" on finding, "*only two or three weeks ago*," that I had the annuity from Lord Melbourne's family, and of his disinclination to continue my allowance "for one hour" after he knew that fact; not perceiving, in his blind effort to prove *me* base, instead of himself,— that his own data confounded him:—that the simplest of his readers might ask,

"How came that which you say you had only known three weeks, to be your reason for breach of faith *more than a year and a half ago*? How comes the date of your breach of faith to be,—not the knowledge of that fact, but the knowledge of your wife's legacy from her mother? How came you prominently to bring forward this matter of Lord Melbourne's unsecured annuity, as the cause of your conduct in March, 1852, when you now assure us, you only became aware of it while examining your wife's private account at her bankers, in August, 1853? You examined that account in order to defend actions brought by your wife's creditors? You were then *already* disputing the contract at law with her? On what plea? Certainly not on the plea of Lord Melbourne's annuity; for you say you did not know she had it. You were preparing your defence without the fact? You learned it,—in addition,—only two or three weeks before the action? *That is your statement*. And that being your statement, is it possible you do not see, that you have proved your wife's case? That you have proved, that the Melbourne annuity was *not* your reason (if, indeed, any reason could justify dishonesty); that her mother's legacy was your reason; and that being justly conscious of the shame your real defence would entail upon you, you substituted a *fictitious* defence, which you thought might throw shame upon her, and prevent, by its confused details, that public condemnation of your fraud, which you felt it must otherwise incur."

There are fifty other such discrepancies; but I will not enter into them; I will not answer Mr Norton's letter twice. I solemnly declare his assertions respecting Lord Melbourne, my mother, my brother, and my sons, to be all, altogether, and equally, *untrue*; and as my sons cannot be expected publicly to contradict him, I can only hope that what is said respecting them, will be weighed in the scale with all that is said (and utterly disproved), of others. I will not discuss his cruel mention of them; bitter as the temptation is. I give my answer to Mr Norton's letter as it appeared in the papers at the time. It contains so much repetition of what has been already more fully recorded in this pamphlet, that I print it rather as a record of what my answer was,—than from the necessity of its delaying the reader in this place. I would merely call attention to the passage marked with three asterisks ******, page 118 (disproving Mr Norton's astonishing assertion, that Lord Melbourne gave him his Magistracy before he was acquainted with me); and I would beg especial notice of the letters which immediately follow mine.

To the Editor of the 'Times.'
    Sir,—On Wednesday, the 24th ult., a long letter from Mr

Norton appeared in the columns of the 'Times.' I did not expect ever to feel thankful for anything Mr Norton would say of me; but I do feel most deeply thankful that he wrote and published that letter. He has now deliberately given to the world, on his own authority, and under his own signature, that history which I have always refrained from giving, beyond the circle of my own friends; and he has thus given me an opportunity of refuting slander, of which I should sooner have availed myself, but that to do so completely, I have been obliged to look through a mass of papers and correspondence; and I have been too ill, since the day I had to appear in the County Court, to make the requisite exertion.

I pass over the charge brought against me, there and in Mr Norton's letter, of extravagance in my arrangements for a home for my sons and myself. The charge comes ill from one who owes me 687*l.*, and who does not even deny the debt, but merely says he cannot be compelled to pay it, because, as was stated in Court, he is not bound by law, but only 'as a man of honour.' I pass the ludicrous attempt to fix my fluctuating income at 1,500*l.* a year, by 'setting' my literary gains at a permanent 500*l.* annually. Will Mr Norton and his counsel pay it, as well as 'set' it? Will they ensure me health, strength, leisure, and the frame of mind fit for so calm an occupation? Will they state what they think my income from literary labour for the present year is likely to be, in the turmoil, distress, and scandal they have brought upon me? I pass the manifest mis-statement of Mr Norton's own income, which I could prove, by my marriage settlements, a statement of his former receiver of rents, his own letters, and my own knowledge, to be nearly double what he asserted it was. With all that 'the world' has nothing to do; and if Mr Norton had confined himself to our pecuniary dispute, there would have been no necessity for public complaint or private sorrow.

The charge I publicly bring against Mr Norton (who has brought so many against me) is a far graver charge than any justice in pecuniary matters. I complain, that twice in my life he has endeavoured, on a false pretence, to rob me of my reputation.

In 1836, I had a quarrel with my husband. Our cause of quarrel was, whether I should, or should not, take my children to the house of my brother, who would not receive my husband. I persisted. My husband baffled me, by sending my children to the woman who has since left him her property;

109

who threatened to give me into the hands of the police when I went to claim them, and I left town alone for my brother's country seat. Such being our real quarrel, I charge Mr Norton with contriving that the whole world should believe (as they did believe) that my misconduct had broken up our home, that I was an unfaithful wife, and that my lover was Lord Melbourne. He brought an action against Lord Melbourne. The witnesses for that action were proved, on trial, to be of the lowest and most degraded class. The chief witness was a drunken discarded groom, who was then a rag-seller in Monmouth-street: both he and others were proved to have been sent down to Lord Grantley's place, and to have received a weekly stipend from his agent while there. The trial was brought in 1836; nevertheless, no evidence was offered after the year 1833; the servants living with us at the time were not called; nothing was heard but the witnessing of the rag-seller and his companions, who admitted in Court that they had received money. In spite of all which strange advantages, and the fact that a woman is not allowed to defend herself in these actions, the verdict went against Mr Norton.

In this present year of 1853 I have a quarrel with my husband. Our quarrel is, whether I shall, or shall not, be compelled to cede a portion of my mother's bequest. I refuse. Mr Norton insists. I rashly count on being certain to obtain a compulsory fulfilment of our agreement; which I imagined to be binding. I find myself, on my return to England, without funds to meet my English creditors. I stop one action against my husband at my own expense. I write to Mr Norton's own solicitor, in the forlorn hope that Mr Norton is acting against advice. I come into Court against my will, upon subpœna, compelled to appear, to prove the debt and agreement. Mr Norton meets me there, in person, and by counsel, once more to raise the ghost of that departed slander, and to contrive that the whole world shall believe (as they do believe), that Lord Melbourne was again in the subject of our quarrel: that some pledge, stipulation, or promise, was made and broken by me, and that *that* is Mr Norton's excuse for his breach of covenant. I rebut that imputation on oath, and by proved facts; and Mr Norton publishes, in the "Times" newspaper, two columns of abuse of the dead and living, including coarse anecdotes of the mother of his grown up sons, which, even if true (which they are not), he himself dates back to the time when we had 'an only child,'—that is, twenty years ago. Shall the verdict not

110

once more be against him?

I was young when this slander was first raised; my children were infants. I was one of a numerous and affectionate family; I had kind friends and a good cause. I struggled like a drowning person against disgrace, and reached the shore. Already these miserable affairs were half-forgotten by the world; and in literary occupation, devotion to my sons, and the firm friendship of those who knew my real story, I thought to have spent the future of a stormy past. Mr Norton has not permitted this. Once more he has dragged me into shameful publicity; but on his own letter I will rest my justification, now and for ever!

Mr Norton says, he comes forward 'as a magistrate, and an administrator of justice,' to prove he has been just also, in his private affairs. In that capacity, and with that view, he proceeds to make the following admissions: he admits that we did *not* part on Lord Melbourne's account; and that before he ever made Lord Melbourne defendant in the action in 1836, he had already endeavoured to establish a case, first against one gentleman, and then—I give Mr Norton's own printed words:—

'And then, respecting one or two others; but no sufficient evidence was found. Then a negotiation for a separation was entered upon.'

In all that followed, he says he was guided by the advice of Sir W. Follett. Sir W. Follett is dead; but, fortunately, has left on record his contradiction of this falsehood, as any one may ascertain by reference to the 'Times' of June 25, 1836, where it is contradicted, on authority, by Messrs Currie and Woodgate. I have also a private letter from Sir W. Follett (whom I wrote to reproach), expressly repudiating the idea of having advised my husband. 'I was his counsel,' he says, 'not his adviser.' Perhaps nothing can better mark the opinion of the trial of 1836, than the anxiety shown by all parties to disavow their share in it.

Mr Norton admits that—(after this public trial, and these private efforts to establish cases against *'one or two others'*)— 'It is true that in 1837 we contemplated a reunion,' and that the miserable jest between us was (on account of my having feared to meet him in an empty house, as he had proposed), that we adopted in our correspondence the signatures of a man and woman, the former of whom had been hung, for luring the latter to his house, and there murdering her. He

111

feels that this requires a little explanation, and proceeds to say:—

'My own conduct, I admit, at that time was weak and vacillating in the extreme. I had loved her to madness for three or four years before I married her, and after we were united she had all power over me.'

I was a very young girl at school, when Mr Norton proposed for me. I was always maltreated by him from the earliest period of our marriage. I parted from him in 1833, and in 1835, as my family can witness, for violence such as is brought before police-courts; and I returned to him on his own passionate entreaty that I would not 'crush' but 'forgive him,' and that he 'went on his knees to me for pardon.' I was safe of his power, and my reputation unsullied, when he made this prayer; I returned, and five months after this letter we were again definitively parted. That parting was followed by the attempt publicly to disgrace me. After that public disgrace, he did, as he admits, ask me to return to him. But that is not, as he would have the world believe, his only 'vacillating' attempt at reconciliation. My husband, who pretends to have loved me so tenderly, and thrown me off so completely, did neither one nor the other. He maltreated me while with him; and he has been in almost constant correspondence with me, and occasionally a visitor at my house, down to the winter of the year 1850. Would any one believe that two years after 'our reunion was rendered impossible,' he wrote letter after letter endeavouring to arrange for our living together again, and speaks of 'shielding me in a husband's arms?' That at the time he alludes to, he was endeavouring to resist my petition to the Chancellor to regain possession of my children; that he then gave his solemn word of honour to Mr Hardwicke, a brother magistrate, that he had not been raising a fresh scandal against me; that he never ventured to defend my petition to the Chancellor; that in his letters, two years subsequently, he begs me, with coaxing expressions, to call in all copies of a pamphlet containing our strange correspondence; and in one of those letters, of 1842, speaks of himself as 'your Geordie of former and happier years!' That not only then, but in all years since, I can produce letters more or less friendly and affectionate; asking services of me; thanking me for serving him; announcing the marriage of his sister; full of phrases of jesting and affection; many beginning 'Dear Carry' and 'Dearest Carry;' anxious about me; complimenting me; asking 'how my travelling alone can be obviated;' finally (for I weary over these instances of caprice), in April, 1846, he begins:—'Your kind letter, written in the good old spirit, which should never have been broken—;' and on Christmas-day, 1846, *exactly ten years and six months after the trial*, and six years after my petition to the Chancellor, he hopes my health is 'crisp like the frost'—praises my brother—signs himself 'Yours ever'—and in another letter begs I will embrace the boys 'for absent me, as well as for yourself!' Is it possible to conceive, that in the face of all this, Mr Norton can so depend on my not answering him, as to venture to print such mis-statement? Is it possible he does not see that they leave him in this position: either he disbelieves these calumnies, which nevertheless he reiterates to my injury when it suits him; or, believing me to be a bad woman, he wishes me to return home? It is indeed difficult to choose which alternative shall save his honour!

The admission he makes respecting the late proceedings in the County Court are as extraordinary as his assertions. No one can read the evidence and not conclude, that Mr Norton broke faith with me, because I broke some stipulation made with him, and that that stipulation was respecting money from Lord Melbourne. I was cross-examined on this point in a manner impossible to endure, by Mr Norton's counsel, who put the question to me five times with little variation, and when for the fifth time I had answered, on my oath, that there was no such stipulation, said sneeringly, "Well, I am bound to take your answer." Now read Mr Norton's admission in his letter to the 'Times':—

'She was quite correct in Court when she swore that her non-reception of the annuity from Lord Melbourne formed no part of the conditions upon which that agreement was come to. I never said it did...... It is true, therefore, that the agreement of 1848, to allow $500 a year was not conditioned upon the relinquishment of an allowance from Lord Melbourne's estate. It is not true that I ever said or suggested the contrary....... The confusion that prevailed at the trial rendered it impossible for me to explain the matter to my counsel; and hence across that part of the cross-examination which implied that a pledge had been given before the signing of the memorandum.'

Mr Norton is unlucky in his choice of legal assistance. When I said that my copyrights had been claimed—the 'benefit of which,' he says, 'she has always been allowed by me to enjoy'—he threw the blame on his solicitor, who had sub-pœnaed the publishers; and when I complain of being all but accused of perjury, he says it was the mistake of his counsel, to whom he could not explain the matter—though he sat by his side, and suggested in an under-tone almost every question that was asked me in Court. Nevertheless, it is certain Mr Norton *did* make this assertion, which he now says he did not make. Here is the printed report as given in the papers:—

'Mr Norton—The annuity of $500 was given by me only on this basis. I would not have given this sum, or one farthing, if she had not given me that most solemn assurance that she would not receive one shilling from Lord Melbourne.'

'Mrs Norton—I stand here on my oath, and I say that that is false.'

The reports may be, and are, in many respects, verbally inaccurate; but that Mr Norton made the assertion in Court which he now *denies* having made; that the whole cross-examination turned upon it; that all public comment and opinion has turned upon it; that it stood as his excuse for breaking his covenant; that it was at once his answer and accusation, in reply to any claim upon him, is incontrovertible; and I so clearly understood it (as every one else understood it) to be his answer to the charge of breaking the agreement, that as soon as I had read over the evidence next morning, I sent a letter to the 'Times,' proving that, as Lord Melbourne was not dead at the time the agreement was made, the stipulation could not have existed. Mr Norton, now says he never 'said or suggested the contrary.' I was cruelly and insultingly cross-examined upon it, but that was only on account of counsel knowing nothing of the matter. Now, read Mr Norton's own account of the drawing up of this disputed agreement. He ADMITS, that being desirous of borrowing the trust-fund settled on me and my sons in case of my widowhood, he found—

'That the trustees could not lend the trust-money without the permission of Mrs Norton and myself in writing; and further, that she would not give her permission unless I consented to give her an addition of 100l. to her allowance, making it 500l., instead of 400l. I was driven into a corner by this unexpected discovery, and I had to submit to the addition.'—

What addition? If as, he affirms in the next breath, he knew the agreement 'was not binding,' and that he could break it at

114

pleasure? And if it could be broken at pleasure, and bound no one, why did we sign it? He himself establishes the reason why; and proves by his own statement, just given, that instead of its being an agreement based on the stipulation that I should have no other resources, it was a matter of bargain for his own interest; and so great did he consider the advantage to himself, that he was willing to give for it (or to seem to give for it) an extra 100*l*. a year for life! In making this apparent concession, however, he says he knew, even at the time, that it was only apparent. He says that I certainly wished to make it 'a binding document, by finding trustees, but failed to do so, as not one of her relations or friends would become for surety.' I beg, on behalf of 'relations or friends,' to contradict this. I signed without sureties, because I received from Sir F. Thesiger (who, at my earnest request, consented to see Mr Norton at his chambers on this business), a letter dated 8th August, 1848, in which he stated that Mr Norton would give me a deed, 'without requiring guarantees.' Nor had I previously named, or thought of naming, any but one member of my family, whom I had not even consulted as to his willingness to be mixed up with Mr Norton's affairs.

Having given his account of the making of the covenant, Mr Norton thus gives his account of the breaking it:—

'I learnt that Mrs Norton had been left 500*l. per annum by her mother, from whom I was not aware that she had any expectations. I then proposed to her a reduction of her allowance, which she would not accede to, and after she had received her mother's legacy and for some time enjoyed it, I did reduce it.'*...... *'I did, in 1851, upon Mrs Norton's income being increased by* 500*l. a-year upon her mother's death, while mine was, from various causes, diminished, propose to reduce it.'*

By his own admission, then, NO stipulation respecting Lord Melbourne was made; and no mention of him was made in Mr Norton's letter to me; which letter distinctly states, that my brother's solicitor having informed him I had my mother's legacy, therefore he will break the agreement. He does not say, 'you have had money given you by Lord Melbourne's family, therefore I stop your allowance.' He says, 'you have got a legacy from your mother; share it with me, or I will force you to share it, by non-payment of what I owe you;' nor was it 'after I enjoyed it some time,' but on the contrary, at the exact date of receipt of my mother's property, that Mr Norton

115

fulfilled his threat: as he expressly says that he did not know, till he saw my bankers' account, that I had Lord Melbourne's bequest—he admits that my mother's annuity was his only reason.

Now this agreement, about which so much has been said, was based on the single stipulation, not that I should be richer, but that *he* should be *poorer*; poorer by one thousand a-year, being the value of the office to which he was named by Lord Melbourne. My being richer certainly did not make him poorer; on the contrary, at my mother's death, the small portion I derived from my father went to him, and not to me. He gives his own account of my previous conduct in money matters, most plausibly, and most falsely; the exact and witnessed truth being, that during the two years 1836 and 1837, I had not one single farthing from Mr Norton; that he then employed Sir John Bayley, who had been his counsel, to arbitrate as to my allowance and all other matters; that he would not abide by the arbitration; made what allowance he pleased; and advertised me (to guard himself from further liability) in the public papers—being I believe the only person of his own rank in life who ever adopted such a measure. I copy two sentences from a declaration with which Sir John Bayley has lately furnished me, in contradiction at once of the whole fabrication respecting my conduct in these matters:—

'*I was appointed arbitrator on Mr Norton's behalf, in the year 1837, having been counsel for him; and thus became intimately acquainted with the circumstance of these disputes. Mr Norton gave me at that time a written promise to abide by my decision. He broke his promise, and refused to hold himself bound by the pledges given'.... 'I consider Mr Norton's conduct to his wife, so far as it has come under my knowledge and cognisance, to have been marked with the grossest cruelty, injustice, and inconsistency.*'

It is with pain I approach that portion of Mr Norton's letter, in which he has chosen to make reference to our son. I think my sons' names should have been held sacred in this dreary quarrel; which began in their childhood, and which their manhood finds unreconciled! My son is not yet in England; nor was he in England at the time Mr Norton states he had these communications with him. I utterly deny that I ever made him the channel of a falsehood to his father; and I deny that I ever said or implied that it was 'an insult' to be supposed to be aided by Lord Melbourne's family. I did say (and

116

perhaps others will agree with me) that it was the coarsest of insults when Mr Norton talked of these affairs *to my son*; that I refused to discuss them with him; that I denied Mr Norton's right to question me, he having bound himself 'stringently,' in writing to my solicitor, never more to interfere in my affairs from the date of the agreement; and Mr Leman has a letter from me written at that time, stating that I consent to Mr Norton's proposals—'mainly because it is intolerable to me to have my son talk over matters from his father.' That Mr Norton protests AFTERWARDS,—either respecting a bequest from Lord Melbourne, or my mother's legacy,—only proves the truth of my warning to Mr Leman, that if it was possible for Mr Norton to find an excuse for breaking his word, he would break it; as he had done to Sir John Bayley.

With respect to Lord Melbourne,—three years after the date Mr Norton himself assigns to the anecdote he has thought fit to publish, he writes thus, speaking of the woman who afterwards left him the Yorkshire property, and who had invited him to dine:—

'I sent her a civil excuse, which was answered a thorough love-letter; indeed it is high time that I should sanction, to a remarking world, your penchant for old men, by suffering this antique faux-pas.'

The post-mark of that letter is August 8, 1834. I do not know if Mr Norton will persist that it is the remark of a jealous husband. In January, and in February, 1836 (that is, one month before our final separation), Mr Norton speaks of the 'unparalleled kindness of Lord Melbourne;' and strenuously urges me to write to him to press the appointment of a friend. I will not enter into the fabulous history of the letters; Mr Norton forgets that as he was then, by his own, admission, occupied on 'one or two other' names, it could not be foreseen that these notes from Lord Melbourne would be important; and the whole of that statement is false. With the exception of myself, most of the persons Mr Norton maligns are dead, and cannot answer him. Lord Melbourne is no longer here to give his word of honour, that the man he served when living, has stated that which is untrue of his memory; but I can very clearly contradict Mr Norton as to one statement, and I do so to show what credence may be given to others. Becoming apparently uneasy as to any remarks which may be made on the affectation of looking with abhorrence on my acceptance of aid, while he himself receives one thousand a year from

117

Lord Melbourne's appointment, Mr Norton asserts as follows:***

'Lord Melbourne promised me the appointment of police magistrate before he visited at our house, or before, I believe, he even knew Mrs Norton.'(!)

And he gives this very plausible reason:—

'Lord Eldon had appointed me Commissioner of Bankrupts in 1827, and when such appointment was abolished by the construction of the Bankruptcy Court in 1830 or 1831, I considered that I had some claim on the Home Secretary, having received no compensation for the loss of my situation.'

Both these sentences are directly contrary to the real facts.

By Mr Norton's express wish and desire, I wrote at that time, not only to Lord Melbourne, but to all those friends, I thought might serve us. I wrote to Lord Holland, Lord Lansdowne, the Duke of Devonshire, and others, to make interest with Lord Brougham (then Lord Chancellor) to get Mr Norton a legal appointment. This not appearing probable, we asked for a Commissionership of Excise or Customs. We did not succeed in this second request any more than the first; but when Mr Wyatt, a police magistrate, died, Lord Melbourne wrote to me to offer the vacant magistracy. On the 18th April, 1831, Lord Melbourne wrote me word, that the Chancellor had sent his secretary to inquire respecting this matter; and had intimated that he should expect Mr Norton to resign his Commissionership of Bankrupts; Lord Melbourne added, 'this is not so agreeable, but still was to be expected, and is perhaps not unfair in these reforming times; and I mention it that you may not be surprised when you receive the intelligence.'

Mr Norton was disappointed, and demurred; he desired to hold both appointments; I wrote again to Lord Melbourne to state this, and received in reply the following note:—

> *House of Lords, Quarter-past Five.*
> *Take my advice, and make Norton write a line immediately to the Lord Chancellor, giving up his Commissionership. What you cannot keep, it is always best to give up with a good grace.*
> *Yours faithfully,*   *Melbourne.*

That statement, therefore, made by Mr Norton, is entirely

fictitious; and if I notice it, it is to ask what reliance can be placed on all the other mis-statements in which blind wrath, imperfect memory, and utter irresolution have involved him? Mr Norton calls his published letter a 'Vindication': a man of keener moral perceptions would have felt, when he wrote it, that he was not writing his *defence*—but his *confession*.

From beginning to end it is a tissue of degrading admissions, or incorrect assertions: of which the contradiction, I am thankful to say, does not rest on my helpless denial, but on the clearest disproof.

Mr Norton admits that we did NOT part on Lord Melbourne's account in 1836; but that he took then, as he takes now, any slander he could find, to involve me in undeserved shame and disgrace. He admits that he solicited my return after the trial, in a familiar, jesting, and caressing correspondence,—even while he repeats as true the gross slanders of 17 years ago! He admits that he had *no* stipulation whatever with me about Lord Melbourne, on this disputed agreement; and he denies that he ever 'said or suggested' that he *had* any such stipulation. Such are his admissions! I turn to his assertions.

Mr Norton's appointment was NOT given or promised by Lord Melbourne, before he knew me or visited at our house, but, on the contrary, after correspondence and intimacy; and it was NOT given as compensation for the loss of his Commissionership of Bankruptcy; on the contrary, the Chancellor insisted on controlling his own patronage, and gave notice that Mr Norton should not be permitted to hold both appointments.

I did *not* put my husband to needless torment and expense by extravagance and actions from my tradespeople; on the contrary, he broke his solemn written pledge with is own referee, Sir John Bayley, and advertised me in the newspapers, as Sir John Bayley can prove. Sir W. Follett did NOT advise the trial, or the measures taken by Mr Norton; on the contrary, he publicly disavowed him as soon as the trial was over, as the letter of Messrs Currie and Woodgate is extant to prove. Mr Norton has *not* proved by his letter that he has been 'just in his private affairs'; but, on the contrary, he has proved himself as cruelly unjust as any man ever was, by meeting a true claim with a series of libellous accusations, raked up from the past, to slander the living and the dead.

I am content that those accusations should be taken at their worth; Mr Norton's word has been too recklessly pledged on

119

matters easy of disproof, to be trusted where evidence is wanting, and nothing possible but denial. I say again, that henceforth and for ever, I rest my justification on this published *confession* of Mr Norton's; on its glaring contradictions in all matters to which it refers; on its strange admissions as regards his conduct towards me.

Even on the showing of that confused letter, our story stands thus:—that after bringing a divorce trial in which he himself so little believed, that he wooed me home again the next year, he revives the slander which an English jury, the pledged word of the deceased, and his own recall had refuted, with the bitterest expressions and false accusations, both against his wife and his dead patron. That he has done this, in the course of defence to a common action for debt; the simple question being, whether he was or was not bound to provide and set apart for a body of tradesmen the sum of 687*l*., the security for such sum being an agreement drawn out formally by a solicitor; at his own urgent request; to procure an arrangement he desired; signed by his own hand; and witnessed by two other persons. That he cannot assert that he had any stipulations whatever with me, respecting Lord Melbourne, my expectations from my mother, or my literary resources (all three of which he gave as his excuse); neither can he deny, that as the agreement embraced the contingency of his becoming Lord Grantley, it was intended to be permanent. I complain that the original simple question has been cunningly lost and covered, by the overwhelming scandal of Mr Norton's false defence.

I resent,—not his treachery about the broken agreement, but his attempt to raise the laid ghost of a dead slander to shame me. I resisted it with passionate despair, because, let a woman struggle as she will, fair fame is blotted, and fair name is lost, not by the fact, but the accusation; and I feel it more now, even than in 1836, because then my children were infants and it could not grieve them. Those who have commented on the exasperation with which I answered in Court, would do well to remember, that I stood there, answering questions on oath which had no possible bearing on the case; well knowing those questions to be put with the express view and purpose of defaming me; knowing the charges implied by those questions to be false; knowing (the most despairing knowledge of all) that Mr Norton KNEW they were false, even while he put them; and that, instead of being allowed to prove the debt and agreement, I was once more being insulted with the echo of the trial of 1836, with as little just cause for the insult.

It is said, why all this scandal for a miserable matter of a few hundred pounds? Better any sacrifice than such a struggle. Very true; but when this petty struggle was undertaken, no human being could have foreseen the falsehood with which it was to be met, and out of which this scandal was to grow. Others, judging where none *can* judge who do not know our history, wonder I did not quietly take what Mr Norton asserts he offered. For that, I can only appeal to Sir John Bayley, and to the evidence of Mr Norton's present conduct. If Mr Norton would not be bound by his written pledge given to Sir John Bayley in 1837, nor by the formal document drawn up by Mr Leman in 1848, is it credible that he would be bound by a mere assertion, that he would or would not place such and such sums?

I have done. There will always be those to whom a slander is precious; and who cannot bear to have it refuted. There are also those in whose eyes the accusation of a woman is her condemnation, and who care little whether the story be false or true, so long as there is or was a story against her. But juster minds, who will pause and review the circumstances Mr Norton himself has published, will perhaps think the fate of that woman a hard one,—whom neither the verdict of a jury, nor the solemn denial of a voice from the dead, nor the petition of her husband for a reconciliation and oblivion of the past, can clear from a charge always and utterly untrue.

I did not deserve the scandal of 1836, and I do not deserve the scandal of 1853. Lord Melbourne did not tempt me then to break my wedded faith; and his name has not now been the ground of a broken stipulation. On Mr Norton's own letter I am content that people should judge us both. My friends have wished me to pass over the letter in disdainful silence, as refuting itself; and perhaps, if I were happy enough to be obscure and unknown, that would be my course.

But I have a position separate from my woman's destiny; I am known as a writer; and I will not permit that Mr Norton's letter shall remain on the journals of Great Britain, as the uncontradicted record of my actions. I will, as far as I am able, defend a name which might have been only favourably known, but which my husband has rendered notorious. The little world of my chance-readers may say of me after I am

dead and gone, and my struggles over and forgotten—'The
woman who wrote this book had an unhappy history;' but
they shall not say—'The woman who wrote this book was a
profligate and mercenary hypocrite.' Since my own gift of
writing gives me friends among strangers, I appeal to the
opinion of strangers as well as that of friends. Since, in however bounded and narrow a degree, there is a chance that I
may be remembered after death, I will not have my whole life
misrepresented.

Let those women who have the true woman's lot, of being
unknown out of the circle of their homes, thank God for that
blessing: it *is* a blessing; but for me, publicity is no longer a
matter of choice. Defence is possible to me—not silence. And
I must remind those who think that the right of a husband so
indefeasible, that a wife ought rather to submit to the martyr-
dom of her reputation, than be justified at his expense, that I
have refrained. All I state now, I might have stated at any time
during the past unhappy years; and I never did publicly state
it till now—now, when I find Mr Norton slandering the
mother of his sons, by coarse anecdotes signed with his name
and published by his authority; endeavouring thus to over-
whelm me with infamy, for no offence but that of having
rashly asserted a claim upon him, which was found not to be
valid in law, but only binding on him 'as a man of honour.'

CAROLINE NORTON.

Mr Norton answered that letter. He answered it by admitting (what indeed he would not deny) the falsehood respecting the appointment Lord Melbourne gave him, which I had
disproved by Lord Melbourne's own letters; he called that
bold, cunning, and deliberate explanation of his acceptance
of favours, a *"mistake."* He said:—*"I had not, at the time of
my writing my former letter, refreshed my memory by reference to documents connected with this point, and in writing about a transaction which happened upwards of 22 years
ago, I was led into this most unintentional* MISTAKE." But he
reiterated other "mistakes" about other transactions, which
happened not so many years ago. He published (to prove that
he *had* brought the action against Lord Melbourne by Sir W.
Follett's advice) minutes of a consultation noted by his solici-

tor, Mr Currie; in which Mr Currie admitted, that Sir W. Follett said, he doubted much if a verdict could be got, as witnesses of the description Mr Norton had procured, "were so likely to break down on cross-examination"; that it would be "important to prove by a better class of witnesses," the extreme intimacy with Lord Melbourne; and that a conference had been afterwards held, as to the necessity of taking *some* step, rather than admit (by not proceeding) that the charge was groundless. On so slender a chance did that mock-trial turn!

Mr Norton also published the opinion and letters of Sir John Bayley, at and after the trial; to prove, as he said, that Sir John's opinion was then at variance with the one recently expressed in my favour. Sir John was in Scotland when this second batch of slanders appeared; I therefore wrote to him; and, after briefly commenting, myself, on Mr Norton's fresh attack; I re-printed this public denial made at the time, to disprove Sir W. Follett's share in a transaction he had expressly disclaimed.

Extract from the "Times" of June 25th, 1836:—

To the Editor of the 'Times.'

Sir,—Having seen in the 'Times' of this morning that the action of 'Norton *v.* Lord Melbourne' was advised 'by the able and upright counsel who conducted it,' we think it is due to Sir William Follett to state, that the action was *not* brought under his advice; and that although he was retained so far back as the 25th of April last, the evidence was not in complete state for his brief to be delivered to him until the 14th of June inst., and when no course was open to the parties but to proceed with the trial of the cause, which had been fixed for the present sittings.

We are, Sir, your most obedient servants,

(Signed)   CURRIE and WOODGATE.

Lincoln's Inn, June 25, 1836.

Sir John Bayley answered my appeal to him, as I hoped and expected; he came forward and publicly contradicted, in his own person, the tissue of mis-statements by which Mr Norton sought to crush me; and I consider that I owe to that manly and frank upholding, the only approach to justice I have ever been able to obtain. I give his letter, as it appeared in the journals of the day.

To the Editor.

Sir,—Absence from London, and a severe private sorrow, have prevented my sooner noticing certain letters which have lately appeared in the public journals, in which my name has been most improperly introduced by Mr Norton, who has thought fit to publish his copy of a case laid before me for my opinion, in 1836, and a letter of mine to his solicitor, dated 9th Jan., 1837. He publishes these documents to prove, that my opinion then was at variance with one which I have more recently expressed; namely, that his conduct to his wife 'has been marked with the grossest cruelty, injustice, and inconsistency.' If Mr Norton's remarks on the alteration in my opinions, had been merely intended to impeach my judgment, I should not have condescended to notice them; but as he intends the public to infer, that Mrs Norton may be unworthy of the later opinion which circumstances have led me to form, and he himself undeserving of the censure I passed upon his conduct towards her, I consider I should be acting the part of a coward, if I refrained from coming forward to state the truth, however disagreeable this enforced publicity may be,—nay, must be,—to any man who has merely endeavoured to do his duty fairly and fearlessly, as a gentleman and a man of honour, between parties utterly unconnected with him.

If Mr Norton's object in publishing my letter and opinion had been the development of truth, he would not have left unstated, facts which clearly account for my change of opinion. As he has thought fit to suppress those facts, I will supply them.

When this opinion of the 3rd October, 1836, and the letter of the 9th January, 1837, were written by me, I was acting as his Counsel; and on his *ex parte* statements, in the firm belief that every assertion he made to me was true, and capable of proof, I wrote that letter and I gave that opinion.

Some time in the year 1837, and subsequently to my letter to Mr Currie, my position was changed. I ceased to be Mr Norton's Counsel, and all previous attempts at reconciliation or arrangement between him and Mrs Norton having failed, I,

124

at Mr Norton's own earnest solicitation, took upon myself the arduous and thankless office of arbitrator, providing that Mrs Norton would permit me to act in that capacity on her behalf. I did not expect that she would ever consent to this, from the position I had held as Counsel for her husband, and the impression she necessarily must have entertained, that I was prejudiced against her. To her honour and credit, however, she at once acceded to Mr Norton's request. I received both, from her and her husband, written assurances that they would abide by my decision, whatever it might be; and on these terms I entered on my difficult task.

I then, for the first time, learnt Mrs Norton's side of the question. I found (not from her assertions, but by the documentary proofs in her possession) that I had been advising Mr Norton, not on his real case, but on a series of invented fables which he had strung together and consulted me upon. Nearly every statement he had made to me, turned out to be *untrue*. I found Mrs Norton anxious only on one point, and nearly broken-hearted about it; namely, the restoration of her children. She treated her pecuniary affairs as a matter of perfect indifference, and left me to arrange them with Mr Norton as I thought fit.

I found her husband, on the contrary, anxious only about the pecuniary part of the arrangement, and so obviously making the love of the mother for her offspring, a means of barter and bargain, that I wrote to him I could be 'no party to any arrangement which made *money* the price of Mrs Norton's fair and honourable access to her children.' I found his history of her expenses and extravagance to be untrue; and that even while he made that complaint, he had detained all her wardrobe, jewellery, and books, in short, every article of her personal property, under threat of selling them. I advised that these things should be given up; but Mr Norton would not consent to do so. I told him frankly, I did not think he ought ever to have retained them. I found Mrs Norton had offered to pay her own bills, and that Mr Norton's solicitor had replied, that there was no undertaking, even if she *did* pay her bills, that her property should be returned to her.

I found, under Mr Norton's own handwriting, confessions of the grossest personal violence towards his wife; and that on one occasion he had kicked the drawing-room door from its hinges, and dragged her out of the room by force—she being then *enceinte* of her youngest son. I wrote to him to say, that, in spite of these injuries (supported by the clearest proof under his own handwriting) I found Mrs Norton 'reasonable'—'tractable'—'very forbearing, indeed, in her expressions towards him,'—anxious to satisfy him, 'for the children's sake'; writing to me, instead of abusing him, that she desired 'heartily, vainly, and sorrowfully, to be at peace with her children's father.' I found that the taking away of those children, had been the real ground of quarrel; and that not only Mr Norton threw the blame of the subsequent trial on his advisers, and declared that the trial was brought *'against his judgment,'* but that one of his angriest grounds of complaint against his wife was, that she had said she 'never would return to him'; that, as he expressed it, she did not 'honestly intend to return to him,' when he asked her; that his sister and other friends had told him so: in answer to which complaint I wrote him word, that Mrs Norton did intend to have returned, but admitted she had said to his sister, *'It would be for her children's sake.'* I found, even while making this angry complaint, and while endeavouring to come to terms, he retained certain pocket-books, and MS. memoranda of Mrs Norton's, in case, if the negotiation went off, he might find in these journals something on which to ground some accusation against her, in the ecclesiastical or other courts!

I read with amazement the series of letters which Mr Norton had previously addressed to his wife, and in which he signs himself 'Greenacre.' I showed those letters to the late Lord Wynford. I said, if Mrs Norton had been my sister, I would have made them public: and I consider she showed great forbearance and consideration in not making them public, when Mr Norton advertised her in the papers. Mr Norton admitted to me his firm belief of his wife's innocence of the charge he had brought against her and Lord Melbourne; and these letters of his, expressly exculpated her from all blame, and endearingly entreated her to return and live with him again.

I then certainly changed my opinion. I thought Mr Norton had done his wife the most cruel injury a man could inflict, and that he was bound to make every sacrifice and reparation in his power. I saw no earthly reason why her children should be withheld from her, and required him to write immediately to Scotland (where the children then were) to have them sent to London forthwith. In my presence, and at my dictation, he wrote a letter to that effect and sealed it. I posted it myself, and thought all was settled, as the sole stipulation made by Mrs Norton was the return of her children; but Mr Norton was base enough to write a second letter, unknown to me, to forbid their coming: and come they did not. As soon as I discovered this act of treachery and breach of faith, I threw up my office of mediator. I remonstrated in severe terms with Mr Norton, and my intercourse with him ceased. The question of Mrs Norton's allowance was not entered upon, as my interference terminated at this point. I deem it, however, the simplest justice to Mrs Norton to say, that I found her frank and straightforward throughout; acting strictly up to this sentence in her first letter to me—'Heartily, and as God is my judge, I desire to make what peace is possible between me and my husband, in spite of the past.' She left her interests entirely in my hands; threw no obstacle in my path; and never once swerved from the promise to abide by whatever terms I should lay down. With Mr Norton (though he had appointed me to act) I found the exact reverse. He abused his wife and his wife's family; he shuffled about the mis-statements he could not deny; he would be bound neither by his verbal promise nor his written pledge; and after a correspondence, which began in November, and did not end till January, all effort at arrangement was given up.

On a calm review of these circumstances, it can scarcely be wondered at, that I utterly changed my opinion, and that the advice I gave to the writer of the Greenacre letters in 1837 was not the same advice I had given to the supposed injured husband of 1836. I gave Mr Norton, on the fancy case he submitted to counsel, good, sound, honest advice, to the best of my ability; and I gave him the like advice when his real case became known to me. If he had abided by that advice, and by his written pledge, the curiosity of the world would not now be gratified by details of his private affairs, which he compels others to publish piecemeal for their own justification. I am sorry, for his sake, that such publication ever took place; and I am glad for Mrs Norton's sake; because I consider there never was a more deeply-injured woman, and that his conduct to her certainly has been marked by 'the grossest cruelty, injustice, and inconsistency,' that ever any man displayed. Mr Norton may attack me with impunity: I shall not answer him; but I will not allow him to persuade the public that there is any inconsistency in an opinion formed on a thorough knowledge of his case; which opinion, now that all the circumstances of

127

that case are more generally known, he will, I think, find to be universal.

JOHN BAYLEY.

13th September 1853
Philorth House, Fraserburgh, N.B.

This letter was considered, when it appeared, to be "unanswerable"; but Mr Norton's struggle was not yet over. On the 24th September,—eight days after Sir John had thus declared the true circumstances of our story,—Mr Norton re-appeared in print. He began by saying, that he had "delayed his answer for a few days, and during the interval consulted counsel upon his power to file a criminal information against Sir John Bayley; but that course (he was advised) was no longer open to him, 'inasmuch as all parties had already resorted to the newspapers.'

Any lawyer would know this excuse to be a false one; and that it was perfectly competent to Mr Norton (if he could have dared the result), to take other legal measures against Sir John Bayley. Declining refutation of the general charges, Mr Norton commented on two only: the breaking open of the doors, and the surreptitious letter privately sent, contradicting that which he affected to write and send at his referee's dictation. He admitted that he burst the doors open; called it a "frivolous quarrel"; and with that mania about money and money's worth, which made him deem such an excuse the best justification he could invent,—gave to the public, as the reason of this scene of uproar and assault, that his wife had bought "expensive velvets."

He then proceeded to Sir John's "charge of baseness,"—and asserted,—not that he did not so act, but that Sir John did not tell him at the time, that he was "base"; that they corresponded afterwards; and that, says Mr Norton:—

> *The period of my withdrawing my confidence from my sole legal adviser after the trial, and as I firmly believed my friend, was when I found that he had become completely infatuated by a beautiful and talented woman, whose performance of her part of a contemplated arrangement he positively refused to answer for, although he at the same time*

128

*insisted upon my performing my part, and placing myself at
her mercy, by withdrawing my children from Scotland.*

My husband is fond of paying me the melancholy compliment, that to my personal charms, and not to the justice of my
cause, I owe, that *all* concerned in these wretched affairs take
my part against him, so soon as they have any explanation
with me! Now, it would certainly have been strictly probable
that any man,—especially a man of Sir John Bayley's nature;
blunt, kindly, and vehement;—would,—on finding instead
of the painted wanton he expected to find, prepared to
struggle for her "rights" and her "interests,"—a miserable,
sobbing, worn-out young woman, appealing to him for
nothing but the mercy of getting back her children (those
dear children, the loss of whose pattering steps and sweet
occasional voices made the silence of her new home intolerable as the anguish of death),—I say it is more than probable,
that being but man, and not the angel of justice, he might
have leaned most unfairly, unduly, and compassionately, to
the person whose bitter grief, and single, simple stipulation,
came upon him by surprise; and that so he might *not* have
dealt as impartially, as good faith with Mr Norton required.
I thank heaven it was not so. This assertion must withdraw
and take its rank among all my husband's other assertions. To
no weak leaning of any man, but to the sympathy of a true
and gentle *woman*, I owe any further negotiation with Mr
Norton after that surreptitious letter was sent.
Sir John *did* tell him, in the interview they had on the
subject, how base he considered his conduct; and dismissed
him with such violent and contemptuous reproaches, that all
acquaintance appeared ended between them. Then, in my
despair, learning the wondrous treachery of the double part
Mr Norton had played, and the end of all my hopes about my
children, Sir John Bayley's *wife* took pity upon me. She did
not know me; I was, to her, nothing but a slandered stranger:
but she came to see me and comfort me. Pure-hearted, high-
minded, and herself a mother,—she strove to stand between
me and my bitter disappointment. *She* did, what her husband
was too full of just anger and scorn to do—*she* wrote to Mr

Norton,—*she* pleaded for those children,—who did not live with him, who were no pleasure to him, who were merely his imprisoned hostages for power; *she* dug for pity in that sterile heart; and wrote, and strove, and wasted kindness and time for my sake. Mr Norton availed himself of her interference, to renew the correspondence,—I have his answer to all those letters,—and his bitterest complaint is, that I had said *"I would not return to him!"*

Sir John Bayley refused to notice Mr Norton's comments on his published letter; or these and other facts might have been stated. He scorned to reply to the taunts showered upon him for venturing to make the truth known; taunts so bitter, that it would seem as if, instead of an English gentleman acting as referee, he had been a Roman Catholic priest breaking the seal of the confessional, or an accomplice turning King's evidence. To be *known*, is, with Mr Norton, synonymous with being *betrayed*. The bugbear of his life is the terrible motto, *"Magna est veritas et prevalebit!"* Sir John had no right to ruin his character,—and his character was ruined in proportion as his conduct was made public. And this brings me to certain passages in Mr Norton's published letter, respecting Lord Abinger; containing, I think, as strange a boast of protection as ever was made by an English magistrate, with respect to an English judge. Sir John Bayley had been subpœnaed as a witness in 1838, by one of my creditors; after having become acquainted as referee, with the real circumstances of our story: and this is Mr Norton's printed boast; taken from the "Times" newspaper of the 24th September, 1853:

> Lord Abinger, who tried the cause, upon a suggestion of my counsel (Sir Fitzroy Kelly), that Sir John Bayley had been my advocate and referee, *refused to hear his evidence.*
>
> Lord Abinger, in his summing up, alluding to one of the letters then produced, says, 'How that bears upon the present case I really cannot see. I myself must say, as a gentleman, I do not think that letter ought to have been put in evidence.

And finally, Mr Norton terms his quondam counsel and referee—

130

That advocate, who ought to have learnt his duty by having been *rejected* by Lord Abinger, as a witness in a Court of Law, in respect of the very matter which in a perverted state he now makes himself a party to publish.

I beg the attention of my readers to the circumstances preceding that rejection of evidence. When the letters signed "Greenacre," and others, were shown by Sir John Bayley to Lord Wynford, the latter expressed himself in the strongest and most contemptuous terms with respect to his former ward; and finally—for the express purpose of being shown to Mr Norton,—he wrote the following note; the original of which is in my possession.

My Dear Bayley,
    I have been thinking of the correspondence you read to me this morning. I am convinced that George Norton can have no defence to the actions, and that his defending them will be attended *with loss of character*, as well as great expense. He should agree to the arrangement that you propose, or any other that can be made. I will write to Grantley to tell him that I have advised a settlement on ANY terms.
                            Faithfully yours,
                                WYNFORD.
Leesons, December 20 1837.

Here then is Mr Norton, armed with the knowledge of Lord Wynford's opinion, that the production of the evidence Sir John Bayley could give, would be attended with "loss of character," and prove fatal to his defence. Lord Wynford's advice was to surrender at discretion. "Don't attempt to defend the actions; the evidence will ruin you." But Mr Norton (himself brought up to the law) thought differently. "Defend the actions; the evidence that would ruin you can be *suppressed*." Two of the ablest men the English bar could boast—Lord Abinger and Sir Fitzroy Kelly—might surely steer him past that dreadful shoal, with this one skilful stroke of the oar! So Hope whispered; and so the event proved. Lord Abinger "refused" the evidence which Lord Wynford had warned Lord Grantley would be fatal. Lord Abinger

131

"rejected the advocate," whose dangerous testimony was to turn the scales. Let the foreigners, whose methods of jurisprudence we criticise, read what can happen in an English Court of Justice—and be boasted of afterwards by an English Magistrate!

Sir Fitzroy Kelly (who, for the use he then made of his skill and eloquence, may plead, like Mr Needham, and the defender of the burglary case, duty to his client and "licence of the bar") represented Mr Norton in pathetic terms, as a high-minded and excellent man, whose extravagant and profligate wife was endeavouring to ruin him by a succession of luxurious debts; a wife utterly unworthy, though the verdict in the trial against Lord Melbourne left her still with some legal claims on that injured and deceived husband, who vainly strove, with mingled economy and generosity, to provide for her and his children!

To contradict this Romance of the Bar, there was in Court, at that hour, a gentleman of unimpeachable integrity, subpœnaed to give testimony *on oath*, by the creditor who was suing for his debt. He could have proved all that Lord Wynford dreaded—all that has since been declared in Sir John Bayley's letter to the *Times*; and had he been permitted to speak, the verdict must, according to Lord Wynford, have gone *against* Mr Norton, with the addition of "loss of character and great expense." Sir Fitzroy Kelly settled the matter. His experienced skill saved Mr Norton. He knew that it is easier to suppress evidence than to refute it; and on *his* suggestion (as Mr Norton has now published to the world), Lord Abinger decided what to do. He simply refused to hear anything Sir John Bayley had to say! That this decision was optional, and not the result of a legal necessity, we may safely presume; since Lord Wynford did not anticipate such a road out of the difficulty; but had advised "a settlement on any terms" rather than run the risk of the actions. That risk was triumphantly avoided, by the refusal of an English judge, in open Court, to receive sworn testimony in behalf of a party unjustly accused and not represented by Counsel! The result was a verdict for Mr Norton; and he was satisfied.

But *I* was not satisfied. I naturally said to myself, "Here is the truth suppressed, and evidence refused which would have decided that case precisely the other way; I have it on Lord Wynford's authority." He advised Mr Norton to yield, to save him from exposure; these other lawyers have saved him from exposure by a superior trick of skill. It seems then, that he is to be protected at all hazards.

Why? Can any one believe that nothing more is at stake than a simple admission of liability for a wife's debts, when such strange means are resorted to? Lord Wynford, in spite of his denial—of the Duke of Cumberland's denial—in spite of his repudiation of Mr Norton and his concerns—was nevertheless the person appointed immediately after the trial to discuss terms. Lord Wynford, on Mr Norton's behalf,—and no other, met Dr Lushington on my behalf, as soon as the action against Lord Melbourne was over! Are we to believe that he suddenly renewed his intimacy with Mr Norton only for the purpose of rendering him that service? Now, here were two more of the chief men of the Tory party, contriving (by the refusal of sworn evidence) that the accuser of the Whig Premier should escape scot-free from the imminent peril of our real story becoming known. Sir Fitzroy Kelly is counsel, and Lord Abinger is judge—Lord Abinger, who began life as a Whig, warmed into a convert-Tory, and on whom (during the brief moment Lord Melbourne had been ousted to make way for the Peel-Wellington cabinet) so many Tory favours had been showered.

What was I to think? Memoirs enough have been lately edited and published by ministers and the sons of ministers, to show the under-current of relation in which public men may stand to each other. If such are the jealousies and animosities of friends, what may not be expected from foes? Unforgotten by me were Lord Melbourne's own words:—"You take these slights to yourself; but they are not put upon *you*." My justification or condemnation, personally, was as nothing. But fatal (not only to Mr Norton) would that sworn testimony have been, which proved that the plaintiff in the action against Lord Melbourne had declared that it was the work of *others*; that it was against his judgment; that he utterly disbelieved the accusation it involved; that he had

133

entreated his wife to forgive it; to return to her home; and had put forward as one of his bitterest complaints, that she said she never would live with him again! That evidence was *suppressed*.

But I tell Mr Norton, on this printed page, that he himself does not know by what a double chance the risk of exposure was avoided; that even Lord Abinger's protection would have failed to shelter him, when I angrily resolved (as I did) to publish *then* the whole account of our case, and leave him to his remedy; but that Lord Melbourne dissuaded me from doing so. It so happened that this petty cause,—pleaded by Sir Fitzroy Kelly, and decided by Lord Abinger; in which nothing more important than a woman's fame and a woman's interest were at stake,—was tried at the exact moment (June, 1838), when, in the first year of a young Queen's reign, the Whig government was overwhelmed with business, even more troublesome than that which the cares of office usually involve. What was my poor destiny, in a session in which a new coinage and a coronation—the revolts in Canada—the attempt to repeal the corn-laws—the conduct of O'Connell—the King of Hanover's claim for his English income—the Irish Church Bill—the first general arrangement of mails by railroad—the visit of Marshal Soult—the creation of a new batch of Peers—the passing of the Irish poor-law—and a hundred other subjects of varying importance, employed Lord Melbourne's attention? What could my sobbing, moaning, and complaining, be, but a bore, to this man who was *not* my lover? What could my passionate printed justification be, but a plague and embarrassment to *him*, already justified, and at the pinnacle of fortune?

Let no one say Lord Melbourne's family should not hold me in kind remembrance: for *then*—young, childless, defamed, sorrowful, and rash,—there never was the day that I did not admit *his* destiny to be the one thing thought of; there never was the day that I rebelled against his advice, or gave him annoyance that I could possibly avoid. I did not even persist—"this can only be a temporary embarrassment by revival of painful gossip, to *you*; it is my life—my future—the strongest temptation of my heart to justify myself." I

134

listened then, as at other times, to the ever-ready argument, that I would be justified *without* these means; that they would be beyond measure vexatious and embarrassing to *him*; that I might "rest assured," that no patience I shewed would be forgotten, either by him, or those above him. I gave up what I had prepared (though it would have been as easy for me to prove all by Sir John Bayley's and other testimony, then, as in this present year), and nothing was published but a feeble anonymous denial, in a morning paper, of the general thread of Sir Fitzroy Kelly's remarks; giving two or three letters from the solicitors on both sides, with even those names left blank.

Mr Norton may say, that since that occasion of desperate resolve—I have been frequently on friendly terms with him. That charge I will not refute. I am but a woman, and not even a very resolute woman. My husband is welcome to the triumph of knowing, that, through the long years of our separation (especially during the first four years of our separation), I wavered and wept; that pride and bitter anger have *not* always been uppermost; that there have been hundreds of dreary evenings, and hopeless mornings, when even his home seemed to me better than no home—even his protection better than no protection—and all the thorns that can cumber a woman's natural destiny, better than the unnatural position of a separated wife. He is welcome to the triumph of knowing, that it is impossible to have felt more keenly than I did, the confused degradation of my position; not in the society where I am received (least there, because there my story was best known), but in other classes, which I have said I do not less respect. I was too unlike his picture of me, to be otherwise than often miserable; often willing to make a raft out of the wreck, and so drift back, even to a comfortless haven. There were moments, too, when I *pitied* him; when I *believed* his story of loneliness and repentance; and forgave without reservation, as I had forgiven before; there were times of family deaths; times when,—as he represents in his cruel letter,—we met by the sick-bed of a dear son, when I thought little of myself and my own wrongs, and yearned to make *their* lives happier who owed their existence to this

135

broken marriage. It is quite true that I would sometimes willingly have returned to my husband; that my son desired it; and till that day in the County Court, friendliness of some sort (if not that return), remained both possible—and welcome.

But on that day, when in cold blood, for the sake of money, Mr Norton repeated that which he knew to be false; the waters of Marah, by which he sought to whelm my soul, made the great gulf that shall divide us for ever! In that day,—when he met me face to face, shivering with the frenzy of mingled anger, shame, and fear, (which he sneered at as "acting")—in that little court where I stood apparently helpless, mortified, and degraded—in that bitterest of many bitter hours in my life,—I judged and sentenced him. I annulled the skill of his Tory lawyer's suggestion to a Tory judge. I over-ruled the decision of Lord Abinger in that obscure and forgotten cause, which upheld him against justice. I sentenced Mr Norton to be *known*; which he justly considers as the deepest condemnation. All secresy—all forbearance—were over, with his false defence. Though I certainly did not anticipate, that, in addition to abuse of the dead and of all family ties, he would, in his reckless anger against Sir John Bayley, himself ruin his own cause by shewing the way in which it had been protected—and slur the very friends who had protected him, by such revelations. "What you state may be true; but, sixteen years ago, Lord Abinger decided that you should never make it known." That is the abridgement of Mr Norton's taunts to Sir John Bayley!

And here I will pause to comment on Mr Norton's angry deprecation of *the means* by which these things are not only made known, but proved beyond the possibility of doubt. He says, that neither Sir John Bayley nor even I (who am the sufferer for life by his duplicity), have any right to shew the real truth by reference to his "private letters." Why not? Can there be a greater climax of absurdity, than that any man should come forward and say: "Ths is a printed, published lie; but you shall not contradict it with my private letters; the lie is public,—but my letters are 'confidential.' You shall for ever hold the proof, but never use it: the openness of an extreme publicity is to attend what I say; but the most profound secresy is to be observed with respect to what I have done." Truly "there is but one step from the sublime to the ridiculous;" and the argument which had dignity in it (that private confidence should not be broken) sinks into the burlesque, when its reasoning sequel must be,—"because thereby the *truth* will be revealed, to my discredit."

These letters—of a mere reference to which Mr Norton complains so bitterly; the contents of which Lord Wynford considered would ruin his character; the explanation of which Lord Abinger prevented, by refusal of evidence,—rise before Mr Norton, the spectre-witnesses of past wrong! They are my justification. In this year of 1853, my husband affects to believe the slanders of 1836. Is Sir John Bayley, on my earnest appeal, not to be permitted to say, "I saw those letters signed 'Greenacre,' written by Mr Norton to the wife he now maligns; I myself received his declaration, that he disbelieved the facts stated on the trial?" Can there be more absurd language held by one gentleman to another, than the strange rebuke:—"Be silent—you have no right to speak; for you were my 'Referee.' I choose to gull the public with a false story; you shall not shew the real story—Lord Abinger protected me from you once before—I depend on the truth never being revealed, and I consider you are a traitor for revealing it."

If Sir John Bayley be a traitor to Mr Norton, many other gentlemen must share that title. Sir John is not the only person who has placed letters from Mr Norton in my hands; nor is he the only person who wrote in strong condemnation of his conduct. Mr Norton persists, that those who have blamed him, were deluded by me into that opinion. This is a poor compliment, either to the understanding or principle of the friends who from time to time have been concerned in these miserable affairs. In that deluded group must stand, Lord Harrington, Mr Edward Ellice, Sir James Graham, Sir Frederick Thesiger, Mr Barlow, Sir John Bayley, and Mr Norton's colleague, Mr Hardwicke; of these gentlemen, no less than five, have given up one, or several, of Mr Norton's "private letters." Apparently all felt, that the extraordinary circum-

137

stances of the case justified extraordinary measures; *all* considered that they were authorized to prove the truth, by exposure of Mr Norton's inaccuracies. The letters so given up, have been in my possession for a period varying from ten to sixteen years; and I have never made any use of them till these proceedings in the County Court. Will others, reading these pages, be able to say as much? Will they be able to say, they bore for sixteen years every species of misconstruction, vexation, and slander, with such proof in their hands—and never used it? Is there any lawyer, clergyman, officer, political or mercantile man, into whose hands chance may throw these pages, who would bear loss of character as patiently? Why should *I* bear it only because I am a woman? In what way is it more advantageous to public morality, that the False Accuser should be shielded by perpetual suppression of evidence; and shame be left to rest, not only on *my* name, but on the name of a distinguished nobleman, a true servant of the Crown, and Prime Minister of a great and free country? Mr Norton comes forward (in his capacity of MAGISTRATE,) and he accuses this deceased Minister, not only of private immorality as a man, but of the meanest malversation in his public office. He accuses Lord Melbourne, in so many words—in the *Times* newspaper—of giving one of the subordinate situations in the Treasury, "*as a reward*" for the subtraction from Mr Norton's house, of letters written to Mr Norton's wife! Is this to be borne, from any man; least of all from a man who himself holds an office by Lord Melbourne's appointment?

At the beginning of this Session, idle rumours and unjust aspersions respecting the interference of Prince Albert with public affairs, found their way from conversational gossip into print, and were made a subject of discussion by various organs of the press. When Parliament met, the most direct contradiction, the clearest disproof, the most lofty and resolute defence, shattered the attempt to render unpopular a Prince for whom England has every reason to feel both respect and gratitude. On that occasion, Lord Melbourne's name was brought prominently forward. Lord Aberdeen in the House of Lords, and Lord John Russell in the House of

Commons, read aloud, to eager and attentive members, a brief frank note, written by that deceased Minister to the Queen, expressive of his favorable opinion of the discretion, ability, and excellence, of her Royal Consort; and of the guarantee those qualities gave, of safe and intelligent guidance, of pure and irreproachable motives, in all advice that might be tendered to the crowned Ruler of England.

It could not be otherwise than a proud and touching thought, to those who loved and remembered Lord Melbourne in life; that even after his death,—past the silence of the grave and the semi-oblivion of a closed career,—his words had still power publicly to serve his Sovereign on a subject nearest to her heart. His letter was held to be of sufficient authority, to define the position, and to declare the character, of the Consort of the Sovereign. What gave those words their value? The profound conviction in those who listened, *that Lord Melbourne had written precisely what he thought.* That with the capacity of judging, he joined the conscience of the judge; that in the sincerity of an honest heart, and not for intrigue or court favor, he penned those lines. His surviving influence, was in the undoubting belief that he had been frank, true, and loyal,—as minister, statesman, and counsellor: from the hour when, with the rays of a morning sun in June shining bright on her golden hair, men saw Victoria mount the steps of her hereditary throne, leaning on his hand,—to that in which, having faded out of life in the lingering seclusion of illness,—no longer the busy statesman, but the helpless friend,—news was brought to the Palace, in the gloom of a November day, that he was *dead*, whose voice first hailed her accession: he was dead, whose counsels, while he was able to give them, never wavered for the sake of selfish ambition, nor swerved beneath the rivalry of faction; but kept the compass true to a single star,—*Duty* to his country and his Queen.

I say it was the firm trust in his honour, that alone gave Lord Melbourne's letter power: without which reliance, these acclamations of a British Parliament must be considered more senseless than the riot of schoolboy applause. Yet this minister, so trusted for wisdom and for honesty,—this

139

authority in matters of the deepest moment to England's welfare—is the same man whom one of your metropolitan magistrates has accused of the most wondrous baseness: and the same pen that defames him, defames me. Are those slanders believed or disbelieved? If believed, where is the confidence and enthusiasm of that burst of cheering, that spoke trust in the minister, and respect for his memory? If disbelieved, where is *my* shame? Why am I hunted and haunted through life, with a scandal involving two persons, but seemingly admitting of but one acquittal? If the story had been true, and palliation were possible for sin, the palliation might rather seem to be on the side of the weaker party. But it was *not* true. He said it was false. I say it was false. I cannot come down and read, amid cheers and acclamation, his letters for *me*: but what then? Am I to believe that I am too insignificant—that any one in England is too insignificant, for justice? Is it only for princes and politicians that defence can avail? Is justification an appanage of position, and endurance measured by degrees in the Herald's office? I hope not. I think not—if this is England, as England boasts herself to be.

VII

I say again,—I do not petition for sympathy; I claim *Justice*. If even my defence offend,—blame the *Law*. If the Law of Divorce were differently constituted, the scandal never could have taken place, of a trial against the Premier of England, which that minister affirmed *he believed to be brought for a pecuniary advantage, and to be supported by suborned witnesses*. If the laws of protection for women were differently constituted, the struggle about a broken contract could not have taken place. If the absurd anomalies in the law which regulates claims on the husband, did not exist, Mr Norton could not have subpœnaed my publishers in the County Court, to annul my right even to my own soul and brains. Had there been no such proceedings,—then, instead of this pamphlet, the work I was occupied upon, would have appeared; harmlessly to amuse those who had leisure to read it. I give them, in lieu of such a work, this "Story of Real Life;" taking place among the English aristocracy; with perfect impunity on the part of the wrong-doer! I invite Mr Norton to disprove it. He cannot. If he had merely been unfaithful, I would have forgiven it. If he had merely defrauded me, I would have confined myself to the formal struggle against that fraud; but he has publicly *libelled* me; and against that public libel, repeated after an interval of sixteen years, I *will* make my final stand. It is not in human nature to bear, without the deepest resentment, the last attack made upon me. I do feel the deepest resentment; and I consider this especial time, when the marriage laws are said to be under consideration, a fit opportunity for shewing what can be done under the laws as they *are*. Whether those laws are amended or not, henceforward those who malign me, will do so in the face of proved evidence against them:—henceforward those who have loved and upheld me, shall not merely say,—"We believe her,"—but shall be able to assert,—"these are the *facts*: and on these, we upheld her."

Mr Phillimore, in a bill brought forward this session, for a very different legal improvement,*—observed that the object of the bill was "*to withdraw from the sphere of private animosity, caprice, and revenge, that which never ought to be left to private animosity, caprice, and revenge; and to see that justice was properly administered.*" There is no question that the principle is a sound one for *all* legal control; and there is no reason why such control should be in abeyance for one particular class of persons, or class of cases. The law compels the poor man to be responsible to the community at large, for the maltreatment of his wife; by a *new law* (the necessity for which has been abundantly proved by the daily police reports). Why should it seem grievous and shocking to make new laws of restraint for gentlemen, as well as for poor men? We have an idol; our idol is traditionary custom; and great is that Diana of the Britons! If we make legal changes, it is rare that we make them boldly. We seldom supersede. We add and we take away. Refusing to reform, we endeavour to compel men to hold that sacred, being imperfect—which, reformed and perfected, would be held sacred without any compulsion at all. It is not authority that offends; but anomaly; a patch-work in the raiment of Justice, so that when men would cling to her robe it gives way in their hand. Now, if there is one law men are naturally more jealous of altering than another, it is the law between husband and wife; yet surely the power of protection is the proudest privilege of Superiority; and in these modern and enlightened days, that privilege may be better defined, than in the phraseology of the ancient law of Baron and Feme, which I have seen thus naïvely laid down—"Now the Baron shall have remedie against one that beateth his Feme—for she is his *Chattel*."

The amount of anomaly in the law on this subject, is start-

---

* The establishment of a Public Prosecutor.

ling; but I confine myself to the notice of points affecting positions like my own.

We will take then, first, the law as to divorce.

The Roman Catholics have one clear unvarying rule on this subject. They make marriage a sacrament. They have laws that apply to cases of dispute,—"separation de corps et de biens,"—provision for the wife,—award as to children,—but the marriage itself is simply indissoluble; lasting, as the words of the Church ceremony imply, "till *death* do us part."

We do not make marriage a sacrament. It is difficult to say what we hold it to be. Lord Hardwicke's Marriage Act, of 1754, declared null, all marriages not celebrated by a priest in orders: and made it indispensable that the ceremony should take place in some parish church, or public chapel, unless by special licence from the Archbishop of Canterbury. Lord John Russell's Act, of 1836, permits persons, on the contrary, to be married according to any form they choose; not sacerdotally; merely by repairing to the Registrar, and giving certain notices, and procuring certain certificates; so as to acquire a right to have the ceremony performed, in places registered and appropriated for the purpose. Marriage therefore, in England, is a religious ceremony or a mere civil contract, at the pleasure of the parties: thus meeting the requisitions of all sects of the Protestant Church. It is besides,—practically,—a sacrament for the poor, and a civil contract for the rich: as the rich break it by application to Parliament; and the poor are put frequently on their trial for bigamy, from not being able to go through that expensive form. It is,—practically,—a sacrament for the wife, and a civil contract for the husband; the husband can break it almost as a matter of course, on proof of the wife's infidelity; the wife, though nominally able to apply for a divorce, seldom or ever obtains one: I believe there are but three cases on record in the House of Lords, of marriages broken on the wife's petition. The law of Scotland and the law of England are utterly different.

In Scotland, the right of the wife to divorce, is equal to that of the husband; and a Scotch lady in Scotland can divorce her husband *a vinculo*, so as to marry again. It is notorious, that

143

the heads of two of our noblest families made a residence in Scotland the preliminary of a divorce of this nature, which set both parties free; proceedings being taken, in one of the instances, by the wife against the husband.

In Scotland, marriage legitimatizes children born before wedlock: it does not legitimatize them in England: so that the same man,—inheriting property in both countries,—would succeed as heir to his father north of the Tweed, and be debarred as a bastard south of that boundary. In Scotland, a mere declaration of marriage before witnesses, the mere addressing a letter as if to a wife, was held sufficient to establish a marriage: and hence those rapid flights to Gretna, which puzzle foreigners; Gretna, not being of itself a city sacred to Hymen, but the nearest village across the boundary of England, that could be reached by enamoured couples. The parties were made "one" by David Paisley, a blacksmith by trade. He kept no regular registry. John Linton, the landlord of Gretna Hall, succeeded David Paisley. He kept no exact registry, but remembered the elopement of Lord Erskine (afterwards Lord Chancellor), who arrived, disguised as an old woman, with a veil and grey cloak: that of Lord Westmoreland with the daughter and heiress of Mr Childe, the banker; that of Lord Eldon (another Chancellor); of one of the Laws, brother of Lord Chief Justice Ellenborough; and of a clergyman, the Rev. Thomas Cator; besides a host of less remarkable, and equally remarkable, cases. These Gretna marriages held good; but the ceremony was, nevertheless, generally repeated according to more regular forms, as soon as opportunity permitted. They took place in great numbers, and it is only very recently that legislation has been appealed to on the subject of their prohibition. The law, the church, and the nobility, thus owe to David Paisley the blacksmith, and John Linton the innkeeper, many of the marriages of their most illustrious and distinguished families. Assuredly, marriage is not a sacrament in Scotland! Indeed, so many strange confusions have taken place in consequence of the laxity of the law in that country, that it was humorously asserted in the Houes of Lords, during an appeal on a Scotch case, that no Scotch gentleman could feel positively sure

144

whether he were married or a bachelor, the knot was so easily tied.

In Scotland, the property, personalty, and rights of the wife, are far more strictly protected than in England: and in divorce cases, she has the advantage over the English wife, in the fact, that the first step is to inquire into the truth of the allegations against her. The English wife, in an action for "damages," brought as a first step towards divorce, by her husband against her lover, is not considered as a party in the suit; cannot have counsel; and can only benefit by such chance circumstances in her favour as belong to the defence made by the man against whom the action is laid. Lord Brougham, in 1838, mentioned a case in the House of Lords, in which not only the man proceeded against, was not in truth the woman's lover, but not even an acquaintance; and the action was an agreed plot between him and the husband, who desired so be rid of his wife!

But we have only to look back to the origin of divorce in England, to comprehend, that the protection of the woman was the last thing considered in the framing of its laws. Whether we ought to adopt the view taken by Roman Catholics, and consider marriage as a sacrament, or whether (as Milton bitterly wrote,—when arguing his right to get rid of the wife who was no "help-mate" to him) persons once wedded should be compelled, "in spight of antipathy, to fadge together and combine as they may, to their unspeakable wearisomeness;—forced to draw in that yoke, an unmerciful day's work of sorrow, till death unharness them,"—is no longer an argument in Protestant England. Divorce, in its fullest interpretation;—divorce, which breaks the marriage utterly, and allows of a new choice; the children of which new choice shall be as legitimate and as capable of inheriting by succession, as the children of any other marriages,—is the established law of our land. Divorce parliamentary, and divorce ecclesiastical: Bishops vote in the House of Lords, and therefore it is to be presumed, they vote on divorce cases: and divorced parties are re-married before the Church, and by the ministers of that Church, precisely as they were before, by a ceremony that never contemplated divorce; a startling anomaly, but not greater than all our other discrepancies on this subject. Our marriage ceremony belongs to the compilation of our liturgy; and our liturgy was compiled, not by angels, but by men: pious and wise men, whose task was performed with reverence, and should be held in reverence; but they themselves prefaced it with the declaration, that it had been compiled as far as possible to reconcile two contending parties in the Church. Two, if not three, of the compilers, were Roman Catholics. Much of the phraseology, and some of the services retained, are Roman Catholic. The phraseology of the marriage service belongs to that creed. The community of goods, referred to in that ceremony, does not exist with us: and the simplest reader must perceive a great contradiction between the Church form and the Protestant law: between the power vested in the Legislature to break marriages on a decree made by assembled peers; and the phraseology of a ceremonial, declared to be "symbolical of the mystery of Christ's union with the Church;"—which pronounce the parties man and wife "in the name of the Father, the Son, and the Holy Ghost,"—and dismisses them with the blessing, "What God hath joined, let not man put asunder." Is it the ceremony that makes marriage,—or the law that breaks marriage,—that is wrong? They do not agree; and solemn and true is the sentence which first meets our eyes in the preface to the Church Service: *"There was never anything by the wit of man so well devised, or so sure established, which in continuance of time hath not been corrupted."* And that because the wit of man (such as it is), is perpetually swayed by the passions of man.

Now, divorce in England, we owe to Henry VII. To that monarch,—profanely styled the Father of the Reformation, Defender of the Faith, Supreme Governor of the Church,—to that King, remarkable in youth for inordinate vanity, in manhood for inordinate sensuality, in declining life for inordinate tyranny, we owe the great chasm which divides the interpreted sense of such language, from the reality of its binding effect:—

"And Gospel light first shone from Boleyn's eyes,"

to enable a false-hearted sensualist to rid himself of his legitimate wife. Bishops were executed for objecting to *his* contemplated divorce; the laws of earth and heaven were confused in the struggle of one wild and reckless will; Rome was alternately appealed to and defied; till on a Sabbath day in September 1532, at Windsor Castle,—while Katharine was yet his nominal Queen and nominal wife,—a sort of rehearsal of a future coronation was made, by creating Anne Boleyn, Marchioness of Pembroke. The Defender of the Faith himself put the demi-circular coronet on that lovely head, which was so soon to usurp the crown; so soon to be severed by the axe! The Duke of Norfolk's daughter carried her mantle and coronet; the Countesses of Rutland and Sussex waited upon her; the Bishop of Winchester read aloud her letters patent of new nobility; and from that day she was attended upon with royal state, like a princess. From that day, for how long? For one,—two,—three months, or more? Historians cannot tell. They dispute the date of Henry's unhallowed union; and this fact only appears clear, that he married Anne Boleyn *before* the sentence of divorce from Katharine was actually pronounced by Cranmer.

Retribution was in store. Soon, too soon, that fair Aurora of the Reformation,—that woman with such generous impulses, such strong ambition, such passionate attachments, such universal fascination,—was to perish as a victim, where she had reigned as sovereign. Vain were her appeals to the tyrant-heart, whose flame of lust being burned out, held no other light to read a woman's prayer by. The echo of the same call which had once insulted her mistress, predecessor, and superseded Queen,—*"Catharine, come into Court!"* was repeated for Anne Boleyn. She, too, came into Court—to be tried and condemned. The lover who wooed her in girlhood,—Percy, Duke of Northumberland,—saw her stand that trial: her condemnation he did not hear: he pleaded illness and withdrew, before the close of the proceedings; taking with him the one gleam of faint-hearted pity, to which, perhaps, that struggling despairing woman had looked for help. She was condemned; by those who did not believe her criminal; for crimes which nature revolted at; for crimes she never committed. She died her death of just expiation on a false plea; she left the child of her brief day of love and triumph to reign gloriously over England as Queen Elizabeth; and she left the rescue of her blotted name, to the yearning regret of her poet-admirer Wyatt, and the skill of contending historians.

The day she perished, Henry took another queen. The cannon which boomed from the Tower, when with patient dignity that forsaken creature laid her head on the block, brought to the king's ear a double signal; of death and rejoicing. He had thrown off the bondage of a second marriage, and he joyously contracted a third. Every circumstance attending that sudden freedom, should have surrounded it with a grave horror. He had executed his wife,—the mother of his child and our future sovereign,—on the accusation of being paramour to divers men, amongst whom was her own brother. He had himself asserted that he had lived in intimate relations with her sister. Her mother had been slandered for his sake: and Dr Bayley in his Life of Bishop Fisher (one of Henry's victims), alludes to the belief entertained by some persons that Anne Boleyn was the king's own daughter. He had sought to bastardize the legitimate offspring of his first queen, and afterwards of his second. He had slaughtered churchmen for interfering with the gratification of his passions, and he now slaughtered the woman who had been his temptation.

Out of that mass of sin, misery, struggle, and lawless confusion of rights, sprung the germ of our English form of divorce. From that date, the power of the sacerdotal blessing stood in direct conflict with the right of the civil law to annul it: and man was pronounced perfectly capable of putting asunder those who had been joined before God. The consent of the Church was asked to that divorce; the pleas held to be sufficient to annul marriage, were set before the Church; but the historical result was, that Henry set himself above the Church; that the primary power remained vested in Parliament, and the secondary power in sacerdotal forms. Law and religion were both called in, but it was to help the lawless and irreligious. The shadow of justice wandered, in the courts

148

where queens pleaded in vain—in the Parliament where nobles bowed their hearts, as they bowed their heads, before the tyrant of England—and presided over the vain consultations of yielding bishops; but its reality was wanting.

Since the days of King Henry, divorce has remained an indulgence sacred to the aristocracy of England. The poorer classes have no form of divorce amongst them. Marriage is for them,—as I have said,—practically, a sacrament.

The rich man makes a new marriage, having divorced his wife in the House of Lords: his new marriage is legal; his children are legitimate; his bride (if she be not the divorced partner of his sin, but simply his elected choice in his new condition of freedom), occupies, in all respects, the same social position, as if he had never previously been wedded. The poor man makes a new marriage, *not* having divorced his wife in the House of Lords; his new marriage is null; his children are bastards; and he himself is liable to be put on his trial for bigamy: the allotted punishment of which crime, at one time was hanging, and is now imprisonment.

Meanwhile, nothing can exceed the ignorance of the poorer classes on this subject. They believe a magistrate can divorce them; that an absence of seven years constitutes a nullity of the marriage tie; that they can give and receive reciprocal permission to divorce, and take a more suitable partner; and among some of our rural populations, the grosser belief prevails, that a man may legally *sell* his wife, and so break the bond of union. They believe anything, rather than what is the fact, that *they* cannot do legally that which they know is done legally in the classes above them; that *they* cannot consecrate the new tie, or get the old one annulled; but must be content to live, paired together, in the only way that remains possible,—or run the risk of being tried at the bar of justice! Nor is this confined to the lower classes: persons in respectable and educated positions, from ignorance of the exact law, or in the hope of escaping its notice, run the same risk.

We have only to turn to the newspapers, and take the first case at hazard, as an illustration. I find one tried before Mr Russell Gurney; so lately as December 3, 1853. I find, in that

149

brief report, a story revealed, which resembles the romance of "Jane Eyre," (except that romance always appears to excite deeper interest than reality). The couple whose misfortunes thus flashed for a moment on public attention, were Mr R. Gray and Mary Adams: the evidence, shewed that Mr Gray had a wife living and undivorced; and was therefore guilty of bigamy. Mary Adams deposed that he had courted her for six years; had no money with her; on the contrary, supplied her with money since his apprehensions; had always been very kind; and that they had a child of his, residing with them. The undivorced wife was living with an omnibus man, and had been in a lunatic asylum! Mr Russell Gurney, in deciding the case, observed, with epigrammatic truth, that "this was one of those unfortunate cases, in which, in the present state of the law, *if a man was not possessed of wealth, he had no power to remedy his situation.*"

Now, if instead of plain Mr Gray and obscure Mary Adams, the parties had been Lord Grayton and Lady Mary, we should simply have had "Grayton's Divorce Bill" going quietly through the House of Lords, previous to receiving the royal assent; and Lady Mary, innocently looking forward to making that forsaken home happy, by replacing the mad bad wife, who could no longer be a "help-mate" to her husband. *Not* being persons of wealth and station, we have a trial for bigamy, and this illegal attempt at happiness rooted up by the stern hand of justice, which pronounces such unions to be tares among the permitted grain, of marriages "dissolved by Act of Parliament." Such an anomaly in the administration of equal laws, is scarcely credible; but it exists; and is murmured against—by the obscure.

This difficulty,—which exists for the poor, on account of the expense of our form of divorce, exists also for women, from the reluctance to allow a divorce on their petition. The first instance of a divorce bill passed in England on the petition of the Wife, was in the year 1801, in the case of Mr Addison, who had lived with the sister of his wife. The late king, (then Duke of Clarence), moved the rejection of the bill; on the ground that marriage in this country never had been, and never ought to be, dissolved, unless for the adultery of the *Wife*, which alone for ever frustrated the purposes for which marriage had been instituted.

Lord Eldon was then Chancellor; but the speaker who answered the Duke of Clarence was the ex-Chancellor Lord Thurlow; who was listened to with rapt attention. Lord Thurlow said, that he had been excited by the bill to examine the whole subject of divorce, and that he was of opinion the remedy was *not* confined to the husband. He laid this down as the principle that should decide judgment in such cases: namely,—whether the parties can properly live together as man and wife? He said—

> Common law and statute law are silent upon the subject, and this is the rule laid down by reason, by morality, and by religion. Why do you grant to the husband a divorce for the adultery of the wife? Because he ought not to forgive her; and separation is inevitable. Where the wife cannot forgive,—and separation is inevitable by reason of the crime of the husband,—the wife is entitled to the like remedy. In this instance, reconciliation is impossible—the wife cannot forgive the husband and return to his house, without herself being guilty of incest. Do such of your Lordships as oppose the bill for the sale of morality, wish or propose that she should? No. You allow that she can never live with him again, as her husband; and is she—innocent, and a model of virtue,—to be condemned, for *his* crime, to spend the rest of her days in the unheard-of situation, of being neither virgin, wife, nor widow?

The speech of Lord Thurlow converted Lord Chancellor Eldon, who declared that until he heard it, he had intended to oppose the measure; and ex-Chancellor Lord Rosslyn also gave his vote on the principle so laid down; namely, *the impossibility of a reconciliation*; on account of the peculiar atrocity of the case, which left no ground for pardon, as common inconstancy might have done. The bill passed both houses, and received the royal assent; that miserable marriage was broken; and the opinion of Lord Thurlow so far obtained that in one or two cases of enormity, a divorce *a vinculo* has since been granted by Parliament on the wife's petition.

Very jealously, however, has the privilege been guarded; and the strange contrast between the laws in two countries which form but one kingdom,—(England and Scotland),—is in nothing more salient than in this; divorce in Scotland, being, as I have said, granted at the wife's suit as a matter of usual and undisputed justice. In what a different spirit the English law contemplates the fact of a husband's inconstancy, we may judge by the recommendation of the commissions appointed two years since, to examine and report upon law reform. In the report made, they recommended,—amongst other "improvements,"—that even the nominal right of petition should be taken away from the woman: that the husband should retain *his* right to divorce his wife on proof of her infidelity,—but that the wife should not, under any circumstances, have a right to claim divorce *a vinculo*: that in short, instead of justice being, as at present (as it always is for women), merely *improbable*, it shall be *impossible*; and that all the gentlemen in England who are so inclined, shall live in legalized infidelity to their wives; the slender remedy left to the wife, being that she may obtain permission to "live apart" from her unfaithful husband. "But the crime of the man is nothing, in comparison with the crime of the woman;" say the objectors.

Why? Because—(and here we come to England's merchant spirit again,—property, not morality, being the thing held sacred), "because the wife's adultery may give the husband a spurious son to inherit!" Truly: and the husband's adultery may give his friend,—into whose house he has crept like a thief, to steal faith and honor,—a spurious son to inherit. Or it may give some wretched victim of his seduction, a spurious son to drown or strangle. Or it may give *him* a spurious son, by some wanton, on whom he lavishes the patrimony of his legitimate sons. No matter! The wrong done *by* him cannot be measured by equal weight with the wrong done *to* him: for his is a MAN, and claims his right of exemption, by natural superiority. As Peers cannot be hung, but must be beheaded,—as members of the House of Commons cannot be arrested for debt,—so men cannot be arrested in sin, on equal grounds with an inferior party.

Now it is consistent with all the discretion of justice, that far greater leniency should be *practically* extended, to a sex whose passions, habits of life, and greater laxity of opinions, make their temptations greater and their resistance less, than is the case among women; and a proportionate severity may well be shewn to that other sex, whose purity is of infinitely greater importance. But to say that divorce,—if permitted at all,—should be permitted to one party only; that Lord Chancellor Thurlow's principle,—that each case should depend on its own peculiar circumstances for decision, and, on the moral impossibility of actual reunion,—should be superseded by the doctrine that only one party *can* be wronged sufficiently to deserve the extreme remedy, is surely so obviously an absurdity, that it will scarce bear arguing upon: and would be only adding one more anomaly to laws, in which already the jealous and exclusive guarding of masculine rights, is often the foundation of most preposterous wrong.

Called upon to give assent to such a law, even Majesty might feel something of the helplessness of sex: and muse on that accident of regal birth, which has invested her with sacred and irrevocable rights, in a country where women have no rights. The one Englishwoman in England whom injury and injustice cannot reach: protected from it for ever: protected, not as Woman, but as *Queen*: as England's Symbol of Royalty: and called upon in that capacity, by the law officers of the Crown and "faithful lieges in Parliament assembled," to complete and perfect by her consent, the power of men's laws. Sign manual, and royal assent, necessary for perfecting and completing laws, under a female reign,—in a country where the signatures of married women are legally worthless; in a country where they cannot lay claim to the simplest article of personal property,—cannot make a will,—or sign a lease, and are held to be *non-existent* in law!

Too Utopian would be the dream, that instead of *retrograding* in the degree of protection afforded by the present code,—better and juster laws for women might be made in the reign of Queen Victoria! That in the exercise of the functions of sovereignty, and the fulfilment of Parliamentary forms, HER royal assent might be recorded, as affixed to those measures of increased protection of the weaker sex, which

153

are the distinctive marks of progressive civilization, as the contrary is the recognised feature of barbarism. The same reign in which the pen of a MACAULAY has defended the intelligent capacty of Englishwomen, might surely see changed, a treatment based on the ancient laws of "Baron and Feme." And the Queen who has won England's love—in addition to her hereditary right to England's loyalty—and who has shown, on more than one occasion, that the sagacity of Elizabeth, and the courage of Cœur de Lion, are not incompatible with the most feminine devotion as Wife and Mother—might well resist, for her women-subjects, that contempt of womanhood, which our unequal laws imply. Leaving, in the blessing of better laws on this subject, a brighter track of light, than all the boasted progress of the "Golden Age," ruled over by the daughter of murdered Anne Boleyn.

In the form of our divorce, (since divorce there is), surely the first step should be first cancelled and altered! Our method of proceeding is,—that the husband shall bring an action for "damages" against the lover of his wife;—then apply to the Ecclesiastical Courts for the limited divorce in their power;—then to Parliament to break the marriage altogether. By a singular form, if the damages fall below a certain sum (forty shillings), though it does not acquit the parties, it implies so much disapproval of the circumstances of the case—where there is, for instance, proved connivance or worthlessness on the part of the husband, or known vileness in the wife—that a divorce would not be granted. It is scarcely possible to conceive a more pernicious system than these actions for "damages." That the form is not *inevitable* as a preliminary step, is proved by the divorce of one of our peers being lately obtained without it. That it can be no proper mode of testing the truth, is proved by Lord Brougham's history of the husband who made this compact with a supposed lover to bring such an action. That it may be a base temptation to needy and unprincipled men, has been proved by examples. That it renders the woman's chance of clearing her character more desperate, (she being already denied counsel or defence in the action, to which she is no party), is shown in the fact that it is reckoned "ungentleman-like" in the supposed lover, to cast aspersions on the husband, which would merely reduce "damages"; and the defence is therefore generally limited to disproval and denial of guilt. So that how the wife has been treated, rarely appears in evidence.

In principle, the award of "damages" is absurd. If the husband be really high-minded, honorable, and injured,—it is a mockery to *pay* him for such injury; if he be *not* honorable, but base and grasping, it is a strong temptation to him to threaten such an action, or even to speculate on bringing one, without any real belief in the accusation: for a small sum may tempt some poverty-stricken wretch to tell a tale, which, if believed by the jury, would bring thousands of pounds "damages." That it is a shameful mode of assessing loss of honor, can hardly be denied. We criticise the custom of Eastern nations, the wives and mothers in whose harems have been bought, perhaps, while yet pure—in the slave-market! They might, in turn, criticise *our* habit of taking compensation in money for the wives of English gentlemen,—when they are guilty. It is a shameless and barbarous form; revolting alike to delicacy and common sense. I know that it is in the usual spirit of the English law, as to injury sustained. If a man is falsely imprisoned—"damages"; if he is libelled— "damages"; if he breaks a limb by falling down your unprotected area—"damages"; if his daughter is seduced—"damages"; if he is deceived into buying a bad bargain—"damages"!

But in many of these instances, the mercantile award seems a reasonable thing. The man whose limb is broken, has paid a surgeon's bill and been laid up helpless; the deceived speculator has suffered actual pecuniary loss; the man unjustly arrested, and incarcerated by mistake, has been injured in credit and prevented from earning his daily bread: in all these cases remuneration is both proper and satisfactory. But the English gentleman whose home is broken up, and who receives money from the other gentleman who has carried off his wife, stands in a position at once painful and ridiculous.

And the Englishwoman—whose fame, happiness, and future, are at stake on the accusation on which such an action must be based; and who is nevertheless told that "legally" she can make no defence—that she is no party to the suit—that she may not have counsel in court—that she is not permitted to state either the circumstances of her separation from her husband, or his previous treatment of her—stands in a position which would be farcical, if misery did not invest it with a bitter solemnity! What a mockery in a case like mine—where all my family and friends could have come forward, and proved on oath the real circumstances of my story—must it have seemed to be told, that I was "no party to the cause"! That Lord Melbourne's defence, and the verdict in his favour, must content me! Leaving the whole world to suppose he *had* been the cause of my quarrel with my husband; and Sir William Follett's representation of Mr Norton, as a fond, faithful, and injured husband, to stand as uncontradicted as Sir Fitzroy Kelly's echo of that description, in the cause decided by Lord Abinger when Sir John Bayley's evidence was refused. The *first* step should be the step taken in the Scotch courts. Let the wife be capable of defence, and let the husband be untempted by "damages."

I turn from the subject of divorce, to the subject of divorceless separation; full of the same difficulty of obtaining justice.

The Legislature, which very properly discourages and discountenances separation between man and wife, acknowledges no legal change in the position of an undivorced woman. To stand the brunt of a vile and indecent action at law, and afterwards reside apart from her husband for ten, fifteen, twenty years,—with every human circumstance, except death, that can put division between them,—does not affect the legal fiction which assumes that a married couple are *one*. The husband retains all his rights over her and her property. If he please, he can bring an action for restitution of conjugal rights; and he may seize her even by force, when "harboured" against his will, by friends or relations. He retains the right of bringing an action for divorce, even in a case like mine. Mr Norton had precisely the same right to divorce me, (if he could obtain a verdict), *after* the mock-trial against Lord Melbourne, that he had before; and it may be observed in Sir John Bayley's letter, that, on my application for some books and journals left at home, he stipulated with Sir John (*even while making amicable arrangements*), that, if those arrangements failed, he should have the journals returned to him, "in case they might be of use to him in the Ecclesiastical or other Courts"—this stipulation and implied threat, being within three months after writing the "Green-acre" letters! So that I was to be divorced, *or* taken home again; whichever turned out most convenient and feasible. I refused to receive the journals and MS. I applied for, on that insulting alternative; and they remain till this day in Mr Norton's possession. So does much of my personal property; including the gifts made by relations and friends on my ill-omened marriage. The law does not countenance the idea of separate property. All that belongs to the wife is the husband's—even her clothes and trinkets: that is the law of England. Her earnings are his. The copyrights of my works are his, by law. When we first separated, he offered me, as sole provision, a small pension, paid by Government to each of my father's children; reckoning that pension as *his*. The principle of the law is, that the woman's separate existence is not acknowledged; it is merged in the husband's existence; hence the difficulty in the matter of the contract. The husband cannot legally contract with his wife: she is a part of himself.

It is boasted, on the other hand, as an immense concession to the wife, that, in consequence of this merging of her existence,—this nonentity in law,—she cannot be arrested or sued for debt. She does not exist: her husband exists; and if the debt be recoverable, it must be from him. I have already shewn, by the curious case at page 96, that it may happen, on this principle, that the creditor may lose his money altogether. In France, married women can be arrested for debt; and it would be infinitely more just to the separated wife, and to the tradesmen who trusted her, that she *should* be responsible to the law, and liable to a civil action; and that a husband should *not* be able to evade the payment of a contract under his own signature, on the plea of the "non-existence" of the defrauded party with whom it was made.

"*It may be law; but it isn't justice,*" is a common phrase among the poor: it is a phrase of which I have learned to

157

appreciate the sound and exact truth. The argument that the husband may be bound by sureties, is useless. Suppose what Mr Norton affirmed, were true, and that the woman could not get a surety? Suppose a case different from mine, who am struggling against a great wrong, with good friends, and clear intelligence; Suppose her, friendless, helpless, foolish, ignorant, and obscure; is she, therefore, to be cheated, by the visionary supposition that she is *one* with the husband, whose only assertion of a husband's right is to defraud and oppress her?

A feature in that "oneness" which occurred in my case, (and I think there is scarcely any result of this anomalous position, that I have not learned by personal and grievous experience), is, that a married woman (being non-existent) cannot prosecute for libel. Her husband must prosecute. When the first attempt was made by me to recover my children, I wrote two pamphlets on the law as it then stood. One of these pamphlets was entitled, "Separation of Mother and Child, by the Law of Custody of Infants, considered": and the other, "A Plain Letter to the Lord Chancellor, by Pearce Stevenson." The British and Foreign Quarterly Review published a long and vehement article against any change in the law. In the course of that article, they undertook to notice my pamphlet and my story; and to prove that it was entirely for *me*, (and most unfairly, for me), that any such change had been planned. The article was full of distorted inventions, which formed a curious contrast with the grandiloquent motto in the title-page of the book:—"*In primisque hominis est propria veri inquisitio atque investigatio.*" The whole history of my conduct, and the conduct of others, was falsified. I was condemned in the most vehement and unsparing terms. The fact that the Lord Chancellor, Lord Lyndhurst, Lord Denman, Sir William Follett, and a host of other great authorities, were earnestly in favour of a change in the law, was entirely overlooked, in the desire to prove a vicious influence on my part. And finally, attributing to me, with the most astonishing audacity, an anonymous paper in the Metropolitan Magazine, on the "Grievances of Woman," (which I had never seen,—which I had never even heard of), and

158

boldly setting *my* name as the author in their own index,— they proceeded in language strange, rabid, and virulent, to abuse the writer; calling her a *"she-devil"* and a *"she-beast,"* speaking of her "non-convicted gallantries," and pouring out vials of wrath in words of excessive coarseness. No less than one hundred and forty-two pages were devoted to the nominal task of opposing the Infant Custody Bill, and in reality to abusing *me*. I read the article with amazement; with curiosity; and finally with exultation. I thought I saw at last, a chance of triumphantly justifying myself.

I sent for my solicitor. I said—"You have told me that I cannot plead for a divorce by reason of cruelty, having condoned all I complained of: that I cannot sue for alimony, because that must arise out of a suit for divorce: that there was no possibility, on the trial, of saying more in my defence than was said,—because I was no party to that suit. Now, thank Heaven, here is a fair opportunity of making my story clear to the world. I did *not* write the "Grievances of Woman" which is thus insolently attributed to me, and indecently reviewed; and as for all the circumstances in the previous portion of the article, you yourself know that they are a series of mis-statements. I request, therefore, that you will instantly commence a prosecution for libel at my suit against the editor, and in the course of that suit, and the proving all his attack upon me unjustifiable, I shall obtain a complete acquittal in public opinion, and clear up all that was left doubtful and untouched in the trial, where I personally could have no defence."

My solicitor answered this eager and hopeful oration, in a few brief words. He informed me that being a married woman and therefore *"non-existent"* in law, I could not prosecute of myself; that my husband must prosecute: my husband—who had himself assailed me with every libel in his power—who, for ought I knew, might himself have furnished to the editor, the extraordinary version of his affairs which appeared in the review! Certainly my husband would be too glad of this powerful and rancorous abuse of me: certainly *he* would not prosecute! Then there could be no prosecution. *I* could not institute a suit. I must submit; and the editor must slander me with impunity; sending out into the world, according to the circulation of the British and Foreign Quarterly, a bold falsehood, embroidered with bitter comments, invented a woman utterly helpless, and already sorrowfully struggling against defamation undeserved.

I did submit. I had no choice. I was "non-existent," except for the purpose of suffering, as far as the law was concerned: it could oppress, but never help me. And the grotesque anomaly of being considered *one* with the husband whose previous libel was the cause and foundation of this subsequent libel—of having my defence made necessary, and made impossible, by the same person; that person still my nominal and legal protector, in spite of the changed circumstances of our mutual relations with each other—remained a subject for leisurely contemplation, and helpless complaint.

The law-forms respecting property, followed the same rules as the law-forms respecting prosecution for libel. Anxious to make arrangements for a future home, less expensively than in furnished houses, I propose to take a lease; and am told, that being "non-existent" in law, *my* signature is worthless. Anxious to recover property left at home, gifts from my mother and my family, I am informed, that being "non-existent" in law, I can claim nothing, and that my husband intends to *sell* them. Anxious to leave what little I have through the generosity of my family, or the gifts of friends— my furniture, trinkets, books, etc., to my two sons, I am informed, that, being "non-existent" in law, it would be a mere farce my attempting to make a will; that a married woman can bequeath nothing, as she can possess nothing; and that my property is the property of the husband with whom I am still legally "*one*," after seventeen years of separation! Anxious to end the apparently ceaseless disputes respecting a provision for me in this state of separation, I accept Mr Norton's own terms, after demanding others; I sign a contract, dictated, corrected, and prepared under *his* instructions; which I never even saw except for the purpose of affixing my signature to it; and I am informed, that being "non-existent" in law, I have signed that which binds him to nothing.

A mock-trial, in which I do not "exist" for defence; a gross libel, in which I do not "exist" for prosecution; a disposition of property, in which I do not "exist" either for my own rights or those of my children; a power of benefiting myself by literary labour, in which I do not "exist" for the claim in my own copyrights:—*that* is the negative and neutralizing law, for married women in England.

Now, that married persons should be *one*, in the holy and blessed bond which unites them under a common roof, with common interests, and in the common position of protection on the one side, and affection and womanly allegiance on the other—is just, fit, and natural; consistent with social order and religious belief. But that married persons should be still considered *one*, without the possibility of interference on the part of justice when living alienated and in a state of separation—is unjust, unfit, and unnatural; and can be productive only of social disorder and scandalous struggle. In the first and more happy position of things, the husband is the administrator and exponent of the law, for he stands in his natural capacity of protector of his wife; that which is an injury or insult to her, is injury and insult to him; and their expenditure is a matter of mutual interest. In the other miserable position, he stands in the *un*natural capacity of oppressor of his wife; injury and insult to her, are no longer a wrong to him; he is no longer the administrator and exponent of the law, but its direct opponent; (for the *intention* of the law certainly is, that the woman shall be protected; and that he shall be her protector.) Their expenditure is no longer a matter of mutual interest; she is a pecuniary burden; provided for with grudging, at a compulsory minimum, on an alien and extra claim, apart from his household government or family care.

That this is a desperate position for a woman to be in; that if she has voluntarily incurred it, she deserves much suffering; that by every possible means, separation between married persons should be discouraged—are all incontrovertible truths. But it is also an incontrovertible truth that justice should be made *possible* for her, even in this false position. That, failing her natural protector, the law should have power to protect. That some direct court of appeal should exist, in which (according to Lord Thurlow's principle in graver cases) the circumstances of each case should guide its result, and the *law* exercise remedial control. It is vain to say, "Let the woman find sureties." Suppose her friendless; suppose her without sureties; suppose the husband to refuse all agreement. It is equally vain to say, "Let her sue for alimony;" she may not be in a position to sue for alimony:—or to say, "Let her institute proceedings for divorce against her husband;" that also may be impossible. What remains (failing these) is the doubtful claim of the *creditor* against the husband; which is, in fact, a side-winded means of establishing *the wife's* claim. It is an indirect and imperfect mode of legislating for her anomalous position, instead of a direct and perfect mode; which might exist—in a court authorized to decide on the circumstances, and award an allowance—and might exist in the shape of private appeals (as many other matters relating to property are already decided). The present method of establishing the wife's claim, through the claim of the creditor, is public, odious, scandalous, and uncertain; unjust to the creditor, and unjust to the wife. The other method might be private, decent, and decisive; and make the wife herself, responsible to the creditor, after making the husband responsible to her. It would be, as Mr Phillimore said on that other matter—*taking out of the sphere of private animosity, caprice, or revenge, that which never ought to be left to private animosity, caprice, or revenge*—and effacing that anomaly in law, by which it assumes power of control over the poor, and for corporeal injury inflicted on their wives, but forbears power of control over the rich, and for injuries of a different nature.

It is astonishing to watch the carelessness and reluctance with which inquiry on this one subject is pursued, and contrast it with our eagerness on other topics. In the Parliamentary debates of this busy opening session (March 1, 1854), no less than twelve closely printed columns of the "Times" newspaper, are filled with eager, credulous, kindly, or bitter, speeches from various members, relative to an inquiry into the treatment of Roman Catholic ladies in the conventual establishments of their religion! Because 2,500 ladies live in a state of religious seclusion or relegation—of which number (though the majority obviously must have adopted that life from free choice), a small minority are believed by us to be enduring mental constraint and bodily penance—the House of Commons votes, with eager cheers, for an inquiry into the whole system; or the purpose of checking injustice and oppression, should it be found to exist. What an impulse to humanity is an adverse creed! How easy to see that oppression in others which we deny to exist among ourselves!

Here are the gentlemen of England, mustering three hundred strong, in the senate of their country; and nearly two-thirds of that number vote with enthusiastic acclamation for inquiry—into what? Into the treatment of women *not* of their own religion, many not even their own country-women—while those very men scout the notion of altering the laws, or of even making serious inquiry into the laws, affecting the interests of their own wives, sisters, and daughters! The beam and the mote of Scripture were visible in that warm debate; and if the heads of Catholic houses should think it worth while to return the compliment paid them, by inquiry into the treatment of women living under secular authority in their own homes in England, I will undertake to supply—not from the vague gossip of angry complaint, but *from recorded decisions in law-books*, printed as precedents for future guidance—such numerous cases of strange injustice, as shall satisfy all inquirers that oppression belongs to no sect and to no condition; but to the passions of men when uncontrolled by the laws which we frame, in a faint and imperfect copy of that serene and unswerving justice, which belongs to another world—not to this!

I speak bitterly! I feel bitterly: I have suffered bitterly. Is it, or is it not, a grating thought, that in a country so eager for justice, the last to benefit by that eagerness, are its own women? Is it, or is it not, a grating thought, that differences of religious opinion should give such interest to individual cases of hardship, that the letters of two young ladies, put into a Roman Catholic convent for education, by a Roman Catholic father, should be read to three hundred members of Parliament as a means of convincing, and arousing their minds to the consideration of one species of wrong; and that other wrongs, touching English justice so much more nearly, should be without even a *possibility* of remedy, by the provisions of English law?

Is it, or is it not, natural, that all the scandal of my own wrongs being revived—and my character resting on the directly contrary opinions of two men—I should seek to uphold my argument of legal injustice, by shewing the facts on which these scandals (by that injustice) arose?

One of these men, is the Prime Minister of England: high-minded, honourable, and intellectual—still quoted as authority by his colleagues, still remembered and lamented by his friends. *He* comforts me in the quarrel which ended in a separation between me and my husband, by bidding me remember, *"That I had done everything to stave off that extremity as long as possible;"* that I ought *"not to be too anxious about rumours and the opinions of the world, for, being innocent and in the right, I must, in the end"* (when is the end?), *"bring everything round;"* —and that *"it is vanity in me to say that my place can be easily supplied, for that no one can fill my place."*

The other is—Mr Norton. He reviles me in the newspapers; he slanders my dead brother, my mother, and my sons; he heaps indecent accusations upon me. At one time he orders *"the chain to be fastened across the door"* of my home, should I attempt to return to it; at another (*by his own printed and published admission*), he kicks the door from its hinges, to force his way to my presence, for the purpose of expelling me! Shall the *name* of husband shield from condemnation one who has thus dealt by me? One in whom years have wrought no change; who reiterates in cold blood at this present time, coarse and virulent attacks, once again to sting me—me only—for they cannot vex the dead. I stand alone now, to receive them; and alone I make my defence.

If, as I have said, my defence be disapproved, blame the *law*; which left me the task of defending, instead of the possibility of *being defended*. Or, if you still blame me, yet amend the law! What have my faults to do with the real

164

subject-matter? I shall die and be dust; but the laws of my country will survive me. It is very fit and fair that there should be repugnance and distrust, when women meddle in these matters: yet no one can feel them like a woman. It is a rule you do not apply to other subordinate groups. The petition of Spitalfields silk-weavers would not be rejected, because they are silk-weavers: on the contrary, each class seeking protection, is supposed to be the best exponent of its own interest.

Petitioning does not imply assertion of equality. The wild and stupid theories advanced by a few women, of "equal rights" and"equal intelligence" are not the opinions of their sex. I, for one (I, with millions more), believe in the natural superiority of man, as I do in the existence of a God. I hold it to be proved, by all that ever has been attempted by human intelligence, in science and in art; even in those pursuits in which no natural or educational impediment would have prevented the success of women, *had they been equally capable of success*. I cannot conceive disputing the general fact, because exceptional instances arise, in which individual women are superior to individual men. As well might it be argued, because a clever child of ten, in a school class, took down his rivals and seniors in every answer, that *all* children of ten, were cleverer than lads of fifteen. Masculine superiority is incontestable; and with the superiority should come protection. To refuse it because some women exist, who talk of "women's rights," of "women's equality," is to say that John Mitchell's exaggerated orations for Ireland, or the Chartist and Rebecca riots in Wales, or Swing fires in the rural districts in England, would have been a sound and sufficient reason for refusing justice to all the Queen's other subjects in the United Kingdom. The rebellion of a group, against legitimate authority, is not to deprive the general subject-party of general protection. Women have one *right* (perhaps only that one). They have a right—founded on nature, equity, and religion—to the protection of man. *Power* is on the side of men—power of body, power of mind, power of position. With that power should come, not only the fact, but the *instinct* of protection.

Even the poor dumb animal will defend its companion and

its young. Even the tiny bird, that pants to death in a child's hand, will resist, to the extent of its fragile force, an attack upon its nestlings and its mate. Power, in its purer form, is protection. Power, in its corrupt form, is oppression. What is the meaning of that sympathy with the heroic, which shews itself in all classes and on all occasions? Why does a blow struck, or a sword drawn, in behalf of the helpless, seem to make a hero of the peasant and a warrior of the Prince? Because the deep instinct of protection which lies in the human heart, applauds, as the noblest and most natural exercise of power, the resolution to *defend*:—whether it be home, ocuntry, the honour of woman, or the safety of infancy and age.

Ah! how often, in the course of this session—in the course of this year,—will *the same men*, who read this appeal with a strong adverse prejudice, be roused by some thought in a favorite author; struck by some noble anecdote; touched by some beautiful pageant of human feelings, seem among glittering lights from a side-box; chaunted perhaps in a foreign tongue! And yet I have an advantage over these—for *my* history *is real*. I know there is no poetry in it to attract you. In the last act of this weary life of defamation, I went down in a hack-cab—to take part in an ignoble struggle—in a dingy little court of justice—where I was insulted by a vulgar lawyer—with questions framed to imply every species of degradation. There was none of the "pomp and circumstance" of those woes that affect you, when some faultless and impossible heroine makes you dream of righting all the wrongs in the world! But faulty as I may be—and prosaic and unsympathised with, as my position might then be—it was *unjust*; and unjust *because your laws prevent justice!*

Let that thought haunt you, through the music of your Somnambulas and Desdemonas, and be with you in your readings of histories and romances, and your criticisms on the jurisprudence of countries less free than our own. I *really* wept and suffered in my early youth—for wrong done, not *by* me, but *to* me—and the ghost of whose scandal is raised against me this day. I *really* suffered the extremity of earthly shame without deserving it (whatever chastisement my other

166

faults may have deserved from heaven). I *really* lost my young children—craved for them, struggled for them, was barred from them,—and came too late to see one who had died a painful and convulsive death, except in his coffin. I *really* have gone through much that, if it were invented, would move you,—but being of your every-day world, you are willing it should sweep past like a heap of dead leaves on the stream of time, and take its place with other things that have gone drifting down,—

Où va la feuille de Rose
Et la feuille du Laurier!

Will none of you aid the cause I advocate, and forget that it was advocated by *me*? It concerns you all. It is a mistake to think that the Laws depend only on "the Law-lords" for their passing; few among you are lawyers, but all are lawgivers. It is the business of the law-giving majority to pass the laws; of the lawyer-minority, to see that they are fitly framed for passing. I quote words that carry with them more authority than mine, words of the late Lord Holland,—to shew the freedom with which an English senator may criticise the opinions of those, whose minds, from legal training, are apt to narrow the consideration of such subjects, to a single point of view.

Lord Holland says, then, in a note addressed to me,—dated 10th May, 1839,—and speaking of one of the Law-lords (in reference to a measure already alluded to in these pages):—

Nothing could be worse in logick and feeling than his speech on the bill of last year. It was, that several legal hardships being of necessity inflicted on women, *therefore* we should not relieve them from those which were *not* necessary, although repugnant to the feelings of our nature, and indeed to nature itself.

Whenever, and whence-ever, Lyndhurst proposes his bill—from woolsack or benches—he will find me on the seat fate may assign me, ready to support it. I honor him for not sacrificing his feelings on this occasion, either to the pedantry

167

of law or the convenience of politicks; and I heartily wish him
success in the bill.   Yours,

Vassall Holland.

Those are Lord Holland's words; and certainly justice is
not a thing to sacrifice, either to "the convenience of politicks
or the pedantry of the law." If this pamphlet be an appeal to
English justice, it ought not to be disregarded because it is a
woman's appeal; or because it is *my* appeal. On justice only,
let it rest. Think, if the smallest right be infringed for *men*,—if
the rent of a paddock remain unpaid, or a few angry words of
libel be spoken, how instantly the whole machinery of the
law is set in motion to crush out compensation; and think
what it must be, to spend all one's youth, as I have spent mine,
in a series of vain struggles to obtain *any* legal justice! Or, do
not think at all about me; forget by whose story this appeal
was illustrated (I can bring you others, from your own English law books); and let *my* part in this, be only as a voice
borne by the wind—a cry coming over the waves from a
shipwreck, to where you stand safe on the shore—and which
you turn and listen to, not for the sake of those who call—you
do not know them,—but because it is a cry for *help*.

I add, in an appendix, a portion of the examination of John
Fluke, principal witness against Lord Melbourne, in the trial
of 1836: indeed, the *only* witness who ventured to depose to
anything criminal in our relations. And I repeat that I leave to
the unbiassed judgement of those who read, the amount of
value to be set upon such testimony.

APPENDIX.

Sir William Follett,—who afterwards, in a private letter to me, and publicly in the "Times" newspaper, disavowed all share in advising the trial (though compelled to fulfil his duty as counsel, by conducting it),—early in his opening statement, made the following declaration to the jury:—

I believe I shall be able to call before you every servant who has lived in the house during the time; who will tell you that, however much their suspicions might have been excited, they never did communicate to Mr Norton any of the facts or grounds of their suspicion, until inquiry was made, and they were compelled to disclose the truth. Mrs Norton was a kind and indulgent mistress; they had no wish to say anything that would injure her; they did not; and Mr Norton had no reason for suspicion until Mrs Norton had left his house in March.

The *only* witness, nevertheless, who deposed to a sinful intimacy, was a groom of the name of John Fluke; who had been discharged two or three years before,—by Mr Norton himself,—for drunkenness and street-riot, on the occasion detailed in his evidence. I give those portions of his cross-examination which decided the case: (as far as his credibility was concerned). He was cross-examined by Sir Frederick Thesiger at great length: I give extracts—

Q Are you a married man?
A I am.
Q Have you any children?
A Three living out of ten.
Q They lived, then, over the stables in Fleece-yard and Bell-yard?
A Yes.
Q Where did you remove to?
A To Monmouth-street.
Q What did you do there?
A I sold second-hand shirts and gowns.
Q Then you kept an old-clothes shop?
A Yes.
Q Had you the whole house?

169

A No.

Q You lived in the cellar?

A Yes.

Q Have you lived there with your wife ever since?

A Ever since, till lately.

Q Mending shoes?

A Yes; and dealing in women's old apparel.

Q Have you been in good circumstances?

A I earn my bread by my own honest industry.

Q Have you been embarrassed?

A I was, when in Mr Norton's service, before I left.

Q Have you ceased to be in embarrassed circumstances?

A It has not been in my power to pay my creditors all I owe them; but I have paid them as far as I was able.

Q When were you found out as a witness in this case?

A I believe about six weeks ago.

Q You were then living in the cellar in Monmouth-street, carrying on this business of yours?

A Yes.

Q Have you continued to live in that cellar?

A No.

Q Have you given up your business?

A I can return to it again: I have been to the country.

Q Have you carried on any business since you have been to the country?

A No.

Q Have you been to see your friends in the country?

A I went to WONERSH.

Q What took you there?

A I went down by the coach.

Q Is that your answer?

A I went down with my wife and children.

Q Bag and baggage?

A Yes. (Laughter.)

Q Have you been living at Wonersh since?

A Oh, yes.

Q Have you been examined about this matter by any one?

A By the attorney.

Q By Mr Norton?

A By MR NORTON, before the attorney.

Q Where?

A In Lincoln's-inn Fields.

Q And having examined you, they sent you down to Wonersh?

A Yes.

Q Does Lord Grantley live there?

A Yes.

Q Is Lord Grantley in Court?

A Yes, on the bench.

Q How far from Wonersh does Lord Grantley live?

A He lives at Wonersh.

Q You have not been living at his house, I presume?

A No.

Q At a public-house?

A For a little time.

Q And your wife and children?

A Yes.

Q Who paid for you?

A I paid myself.

Q Who gave you the money?

A The solicitor gave me money to pay my fare.

Q How much money?

A About 10£. (*The "fare" is from London to Guildford.*)

Q Did he give you the 10£ before you went to Wonersh?

A Yes.

Q Has he not given you any since?

A No.

Q You are sure of it?

A Yes.

Q You gave up your business and went to Wonersh?

A Yes.

Q When did you leave Wonersh?

A Last night.

Q How long did you live at the public-house?

A About a week.

Q What public-house?

A The Grantley Arms.

Q Did you carry on any business at Wonersh?

A No.

Q And you lived in that lodging up to last night?

A Yes.

Q How have you been employed?

A *I amused myself as well as I could.*

Q Did you go out fishing or shooting?

A I *have gone out fishing.* (Laughter.)

Q How else did you amuse yourself?

A I walked about and exerted myself as well as I could.

Q Did you ever see Lord Grantley?
A Twice while I was there, and spoke to him once.

* * * * * * *

Q Have you not said that you were under examination for nine days?
A I did not say under examination; but I went to the solicitor's chambers every day; sometimes I was examined, and sometimes I was not.
Q But have you not said that you were under examination for nine days?
A Not to my recollection.
Q Will you swear you have not said so?
A Not to my recollection.
Q Try to recollect.
A I cannot; I might have said so, but I cannot *recollect*.
Q Have you not said that Lord Wynford examined you?
A Never in my life; I do not know Lord Wynford.

* * * * * * *

Q I ask you upon your oath, have you not said, that although Lord Wynford examined you, he did not know what you would say?
A I do not *recollect* anything of the kind, or that I did say anything of the kind.
Q Will you swear positively that you did not say so?
A I cannot say, but I cannot *recollect*.
Q I will once more put the question about the 500*l*. or 600*l*. Will you swear that you have not said that after the trial was done you would get 500*l*.?
A How could I say such a thing?
Q Will you swear that you have not said so?
A I never *recollect* of having said it.
Q Will you swear that you have not said so?
A I never *recollect* saying so.
Q From whom did you buy that cab, and the fly, and the gig?
A One from one man, the other from another.
Q From whom did you get the cab?
A A man of the name of Saunders built my cab.
Q Have you paid him for it?
A There was a settlement between us. I really don't know how I stand.

172

Q You don't know! Have you paid for the gig?

A The gig was included in the account to me for the cab.

Q From whom did you buy the fly?

A I bought the fly from a man of the name of Crook.

Q Have you paid him?

A I paid him part, and I owe him part.

Q Well, then, you have sold the cab, and the gig, and the fly; will you swear that you have paid for any of them?

A I have paid part.

Q Have not you said that after the trial was over, you would get 500*l.* or 600*l.* a-year?

A Oh dear! Sir, I only wish I may get enough to eat or drink, much less 500*l.*

Q But I ask you if you have said so?

A Oh no. I came forward with a free good will, and to speak the truth.

Q No doubt; but I asked you if you had not said that after the trial you would get 500*l.*?

A I do not *recollect* anything of the kind.
By the COURT.—Do you wish to say that you did not say so, or that you do not recollect having said so?

A I do not *recollect* ever saying it. I might have said it, but I am sure I could not have said it.

Q How could you not have said it?

A Oh I am not acquainted with the law. I don't know what gentlemen give. I don't know anything. *I don't know what is given.* I don't know anything about it.

Q Have you not said to Sly that you were employed to fish out evidence?

A I might have said I was going after a fellow-servant.

Q I give you the very words: did you not say you were employed to fish for evidence?

A I might have said I was going after a witness for Mr Norton.

Q I will have my words answered, if you please.

A I do not think I said, *to fish up all the evidence.* I might have said I was employed to go after my fellow-servants.

Q You have said you sometimes went a-fishing. Probably this was the kind of fishing you liked best?

A I did not say I was employed to fish up the evidence. I deny the expression. I say, I might say I was going after my fellow-servant as a witness.

Q Might you not have said you were employed to fish up evidence, although you do not recollect it?

173

A No, I do not *recollect* it.

Q But you might have said so?

A I might have said so; but I do not think I have said so.

Q Did you not say to Sly, that you had been suffering a good deal of late years, and that you thought this matter would make you amends?

A No; I only said I had been out of place two years. I was obliged to work at mending shoes. Of course a man must work if he means to get a bit of bread. I always did work, and very laboriously too.

Q Well, did you say you had been out of place, and that this matter would make amends to you?

A No. I might have done; but I do not *recollect* saying so.

Q But you might have done it?

A I do not *recollect* saying so. What I recollect I will answer, and what I don't recollect I cannot answer.

Q Will you swear that you did not say to Sly, that this business would make you amends?

A I cannot swear that I did *not* say so, and cannot swear that I *did*. The fact is, about making amends, I do not understand at all myself, what amends a man can have for speaking the truth.

Q Did you not say to Sly, that you intended to take care of yourself?

A To take care of myself! I hope I shall always take care of myself (laughter).

Q Very well. Therefore it is not unlikely you did say you intended to take care of yourself?

A If I had not looked more to others than to myself, I should not be so badly off.

Q Did not you say, that most likely you would be able to leave London, and retire to the country after this trial?

A No.

Q No, upon your oath?

A I have already said, I cannot say I said so, since I do not *recollect* that I ever said so.

By the COURT: You were asked if you did not say you would most probably be able to retire to the country after this trial?

A I do not *recollect*, and how can I say what I do not recollect?

Q Will you *swear* you did not say so?

A I think I might have been able to go down to the country, for I was getting on very well in Monmouth-street.

Q You were going on very comfortably in the cellar?

A I was paying my way.

Q Will you SWEAR that you have not said, that after the trial was over you would get 500*l*. or 600*l*., and would retire to Scotland, and

174

would not care for anything?

A I don't *recollect* anything of the kind. I cannot swear I may not have said so. I do not believe I ever said anything of the kind, but I can't swear. I have sworn already to speak the truth, but I do not *recollect* anything of the kind.

Q Now, sir, again upon your solemn oath, I ask, have you not used these words, or words to this effect—that, if all went on right, you would have 500*l.* or 600*l.*, and retire to Scotland, and not care for anybody?

A Never, *to my knowledge.*

Q Never, to your knowledge? That is the only answer you can give me?

A Never, to my knowledge.

Q Have not you said so within the last fortnight?

A Never, to my knowledge.

Q Have you said so within a week?

A Never, to my knowledge.

Q Have you said so within the last 48 hours?

A Never, to my knowledge.

Q Have you said so within the last 24 hours?

A Not to my knowledge.

*   *   *   *   *   *   *

Q How was it that you left Mr Norton's?

A To tell the truth, I got a drop too much (laughter). It was a Court-day, and we generally have a drop at such a time. Mr and Mrs Norton fell out in the carriage, and of course they put the spite upon me, and so I was discharged (laughter).

Q Then you had got a drop too much?

A Why, I like to speak the truth, and I confess I had (laughter). Mrs Norton was very cross, and you could not please her very easily. She was cross because the black horse happened to gallop, and I could not get him into a trot; horses will break sometimes, you can't help it (laughter).

Q. And they put the spite on you?

A Oh, it is not the first time I have had it like that.

Q You like to speak the truth sometimes; you took a drop too much, eh?

A I don't know who does not at times. We are all alike for that, masters and servants (great laughter).

Q Did not Mrs Norton complain that you had drunk too much?

175

A Mrs Norton never complained of that, because I was a good servant, though I did take a drop too much; a very good servant, and you know gentlemen do the same sometimes.

Q Have you not had a sabre cut in your head!

A No, thank God; but I had a touch on my hip at Waterloo.

Q How often did you take a drop too much, while in Mr Norton's service?

A What, Sir, during the four years? (great laughter). You have put a very heavy question.

Q But on a moderate computation?

A Why, some people carry a little so well, that you can't tell when they've got a drop too much. I can't answer your question.

Q Did it not happen generally in the afternoon?

A I was not drunk. Sir, every day (laughter).

Q But pretty often?

A Middling; as we generally all are.

Q Did it ever happen that you had taken too much when driving Mr and Mrs Norton to the Queen's ball?

A I was sober going to the Queen's ball; but when going to the Marquis of Lansdowne's in the evening I certainly got a drop too much; and then the black horse began to gallop. Mr Norton got out of the coach, and mounted the box in his opera-hat, and I did not think he looked well driving in that fashion (laughter).

Q You were so drunk that it was necessary for Mr Norton to get on the coach-box with his opera-hat to drive?

A I'll tell you the whole, Sir. When Mrs Norton wanted Mr Norton to do anything, he was so fond of her he would do it, let it be what it might. So he got upon the box, and I, being a goodish sort of a coachman, did not wish to see my master make a fool of himself in a crowd; so I said, 'If you will drive you must drive by yourself.' I had one of my own, and one of my master's horses, in the carriage, and I did not like to see my own horse doing all the work, so I preferred walking; a pretty good proof that I was not very drunk (laughter). When I got to the Marquis of Lansdowne's I expected to see the carriage at the door; but instead of that I saw a parcel of fellows cutting at my horse. I then said to my master, 'Let me drive, and I will soon get you up. The truth is,' says I, 'you look rather foolish;' but he refused to give up the reins, and I then said, 'If you will be obstinate, I must take *my* horse out' (roars of laughter). So I went to take my horse out, and Mr Norton said, 'John, John, don't do that—policeman, take John away' (great laughter). I did not take the horse out, but a policeman came up and said that I must go along with him. I said, 'I am very willing to go with you, my good fellow; I will go with all the pleasure in the world.' So he took me to the watchhouse.

Q Poor John! And so there you were locked up all night?

A I was.

Q Did you not make an offer to release him then?

A I wanted to take hold of the reins, to get him out of the crowd.

Q Did Mr Norton contrive to get the carriage up, driving with his opera hat on?

A So I understood the next morning.

Q And then you were discharged?

A I was fined 5*s*. for being intoxicated at the office, though I was then as sober as I am now.

Q Who was the magistrate who fined you 5*s*.?

A Mr Norton seemed to know him, for they talked together a long while.

Q Then you think your sentence was a very unjust one?

A I don't think I was well used.

Q You were not drunk?

A No, when I went away with the policeman, no more than I am now.

Q It was very unjust, then, that you were turned off?

A Oh, Sir, when Mrs Norton told master to do anything, he must do it.

Q It was her fault, then, was it not?

A Rather more her's than master's.

Q Now, did you not say that that d—d b—h, Mrs Norton, had got you discharged?

A I do not *recollect* whether I did or not, but I may have said it. I had had my wife confined, I lost my business, and it was enough to make any man angry, and speak what he did not mean.

Q Did not you say that you would be revenged on her, or something of that sort?

A No, never, never.

Q What, never?

A I did not.

Q Have you not said that you were the principal witness against the Premier of England?

A No. I might have said I was one of them, but there was a good many of them.

Q But you might have said you were the principal witness against the Premier?

A The Premier of England! I never did.

Q Have you not said they forced you to leave your shop in

177

Monmouth-street, and go to Wonersh?

A I did not say there was any *forcing* in it.

Q Have you not said they took you away at a moment's notice?

A I don't think I have.

Q Did you not say you were to remain at Wonersh, and not to come to London till the trial came on?

A I *did* stop there. I remained there till last night.

Another witness having also deposed to receiving money, and remaining resident, with all her family, at Wonersh, for some weeks before the trial, the Attorney-General commented on these extraordinary admissions in his reply. He said—

His learned friend (Sir William Follett) had promised the jury to call before them all the persons who had been in the service of Mr and Mrs Norton. But had he performed that promise?—*All* the witnesses had not been called; the evidence had been garbled; and those witnesses alone had been called, who had previously been tutored as to the evidence they were to give.

* * * * * * *

The witness Fluke, was the one who boasted he was the principal witness against the Premier of England, and said, 'if all went well he should make 600*l*., and spend the rest of his days in ease in Scotland.' It seemed he had been a soldier, and fought at Waterloo. When he came into the service of Mr Norton he had a cab, a gig, and a fly. He acknowledged he had been often drunk. He left the plaintiff's service in debt, and swindled several people. He bought the fly from Saunders to turn it into money, for he sold it. He had a colt to break in, which he sold for 20*l*., and no part of the money did he pay to the owner of the colt. He then went to Sloane-street, sold the cab, and then took a cellar in Monmouth-street, where he set up as a dealer in old clothes, where he remained until he was ready to sell himself as a witness; and a glorious day it was for him when he was discovered. From such evidence as this, was the plaintiff's case made up! Fluke said he expected to be paid, because '*does not every man expect to be paid?*' He (the Attorney-General) had a great curiosity to know if he did not expect 500*l*. or 600*l*., and repeatedly asked him. All he said was 'I do not *recollect*,' ('*non mi ricordo*,') repeated at least ten times. He (the Attorney-General) asked him if he had not, within the last 48 hours, said that he expected to make 500*l*.? He would only say he 'could not *recollect*.' He *did* recollect that he got so drunk on taking Mr and Mrs Norton to Lansdowne house, that Mr Norton got on the box and drove the carriage;

178

whereupon he (Fluke) ran to Lansdowne house, and endeavoured to unharness and take away one of the horses, which he said was his own; and his behaviour was so violent that he was taken to the watch house! Would the jury act upon the testimony of such a man—would they hang a dog upon it? If he had *not* said 'that if there was a verdict he should get 500*l*.,' he would immediately and positively have denied that he had ever used such words; but he did not dare to give a direct denial; he merely said he 'did not *recollect*,' and it was not possible to call witnesses to contradict such testimony. He took care to avoid the possibility of being contradicted, or of being indicted for perjury. This was the expedient of a deceitful and artful witness; but he would ask the jury if they had any doubt that he DID say so; aye, twenty times! Coupling this answer, 'that he did not *recollect*, with his swindling, drunkenness, and history, could the jury place the smallest reliance on his testimony? Why did they send him to Wonersh? For six weeks he had been disporting himself at Wonersh, fishing, and talking over his evidence with Mrs Comyns, and considering how he should secure ease for the remainder of his life.....
Why were not those witnesses who were living in the service when the separation took place, produced before the jury? Not only were they not produced, but those who had been in the service during the years 1834, 1835, and 1836, were kept back. All those persons had been examined out of court; but it appeared that only those who would answer the whip, and had such convenient memories as to be able to recollect things which were said to have taken place years ago,—but had forgot what had occurred within the last 48 hours,— were selected...

There was a charge against two parties, and they should bear this in mind, that neither of them could be called as witnesses. Lord Melbourne could not, because he was the defendant—Mrs Norton could not, because she was the wife of the plaintiff. Therefore it was impossible, if any witness could come forward and say that he had seen a fact, when no persons except those two were present, that that witness could be contradicted. They could only, in such a case, look to the character of the witness, the probability of the story, and the credit to which it was entitled. If a charge of want of chastity was brought against the purest of women, and that no one but the accuser was said to be present, she must rest her defence on her own innocence, the improbability of the story, and the character of the accuser...

In the Ecclesiastical Court, time, and place, and circumstance, must be proved; but here, there was nothing definitive; the evidence ranging over a period of four or five years, and excluding all evidence of what occurred within the last two or three years........ What family, he would ask, could be safe, if at the distance of years, discarded servants could come forward and make such statements, concealed for so long a period, and which they themselves admit excited no suspicion while the circumstances were recent, and while they were there to make their observations? If they were to be brought forward at the end of years,—excited with the hopes of reward, and of making their fortunes,—what safety could there be, what protection for innocent persons? He could not approve of the manner in which the witnesses had been carried off from their homes to Wonersh. He cared not who was offended, but he would say, that the system of carrying off the witnesses, such as had been detailed that day—of giving them large sums of money—of exciting these extravagant expectations, that had been detailed, *if their evidence proved successful*—was one which could not be defended, and was a mode of conducting a case, reflecting very little credit on those resorting to it. No case had ever been conducted as the present had been...... It was the duty of the plaintiff to have laid before them the circumstances under which the quarrel and separation had taken place between Mr and Mrs Norton; when it might have been seen to demonstration, that Lord Melbourne had no more concern in the matter than any indifferent bystander then in Court; that bringing such a charge against Lord Melbourne was a mere after-thought; that it was what had never entered into the head of Mr Norton himself, but was put into his head by others; he would not say WHO,—he would not insinuate who,—but it must have been some insinuating rogue who had devised the slander.

It had been asserted that every servant in the service of Mr Norton would be produced: but Mrs Gulliver, whose testimony was most material, had been withheld. If truth only was the object of the other party, why had she not been produced? And why had not Fitness been called, who was at that moment living at Storey's Gate? They had not dared to call him, because he was there at the time of the separation; and if it had not been that Mrs Morris had been called to prove the handwriting of Mrs Norton, the circumstances which led to the separation would have remained a secret and a mystery. Nay, it would have been left for them to surmise, that Mr Norton had actually separated from his wife in consequence of discovering her intimacy with Lord Melbourne. But what was the fact, as it now appeared from the questions he had put to the witness Mrs Morris? Why, that a quarrel had taken place between them on account of the proposed visit to Frampton; and that in consequence of that, Mr Norton gave orders that the children should be kept at home, and

180

then sent them first to Berkeley-street, and afterwards to Wonersh; and Mrs Norton was thrown into the deepest consternation, and almost into a state of distraction, at finding that her children were to be thus separated from her. She pursued them all over the town, until she found them in Berkeley-street—where her tears and entreaties to see them were unavailing.... But it is quite clear that some persons have made Mr Norton a tool—an instrument of shame—he has been persuaded to allow his name to be used; and used merely for party and political purposes. Before I sit down, gentlemen, I think it right, in the name of Lord Melbourne, to declare, as he instructed me to do—in the most CLEAR, EMPHATIC, and SOLEMN MANNER—that he never had criminal intercourse with Mrs Norton, nor did he ever do anything in the slightest degree to abuse the confidence which her husband reposed in him. I allow that you must find your verdict according to the evidence, and that you must not allow yourselves to be swayed by the solemn declaration of Lord Melbourne. You must look to the evidence—I wish you to do so—but looking at the evidence, I say that it is IMPOSSIBLE to find a verdict for the Plaintiff.".…

The Learned Judge summed up at some length.

The Jury having turned round, and conferred a few seconds,

The foreman said,—"My lord, we are agreed; it is my duty to say that our verdict is for the Defendant."

The announcement was received with loud bursts of applause.

A few days afterwards, Sir W. Follett thus deprecated the notion that he had countenanced the proceedings which he conducted as counsel: and thus publicly disowned Mr Norton's cause. So much for the great scandals by which a woman's whole destiny may be darkened and wrecked!—*See* p.

PREFACE

to original edition 1854

IT has been remarked to me, that if there were no other reason why a very reluctant attention should be granted to this Pamphlet, there would be "*no time*" to notice a discussion of the Law, arising out of affairs purely personal, at a period when subjects of momentous public importance occupy the minds of all men. In answer to that remark, I can only say, that I have never yet seen the public mind in a state of such undivided attention. I have no doubt, that in the present Session, as in all others, there will be "time" for all usual employments; time for assemblies, operas, and balls; time for races, club-dinners, and *fêtes*; time for reading works of science, and works of fiction; for the most abstract study, and for the most frivolous gossip; time to discuss whether the arms of Scotland are properly quartered with the arms of England, as well as to debate whether the Emperor of Russia is to make war upon the world. It would be paying Englishmen a poor compliment to suppose that the one subject they are determined *not* to find time for, is the reform of some of their own laws; a reform confidently alluded to by the Lord Chancellor, in his speech of the 14th February last year; and formally introduced as one of the topics of the Queen's Speech at the opening of Parliament.

Lord Campbell—in his brilliant and interesting work, "The Lives of the Chancellors"—tells us that in the session of 1758 reference was made to the Judges on the motion of Ex-Chancellor Hardwicke, respecting a bill for amending the law of Habeas Corpus; and it was proposed to introduce a new bill in the ensuing session. "But I am sorry to say,"—observes Lord Campbell,—"that when the next session arrived, nothing was thought of except the taking of QUEBEC; and the subject was not again resumed, till the very close of the reign of George III."

Now it is certainly possible, that in like manner the Law reforms so confidently promised for this session, may be set aside; and some future writer of Chancellors' Lives, may express his regret, that "in the Session of 1854 little was thought of except the taking of SEBASTOPOL."

But, if another half century should glide away without reform in our Ecclesiastical and other Courts (as more than half a century elapsed, between the motion of Ex-Chancellor Hardwicke and the amendment of the Habeas Corpus Act) shall we set it all down to the overwhelming interest taken in Quebec and Sebastopol?

Shall we not rather look for the solution of these delays, in a certain supineness on the part of those who work the machinery of justice? and in the fact (also stated by Lord Campbell) that "it is very difficult to draw the notice of the representatives of the people to measures for the Amendment of the Law." Difficult to draw attention to such measures; not difficult to find "time," either for their discussion, or the consideration of any examples which may prove the necessity of change.